UNPACKING A *TRADITIONAL* CHRISTMAS

Unpacking a Traditional Christmas: 25 Songs and Stories for the Season
Copyright © 2023 Mark Hecht & Janet Lord

All rights reserved. No part of this publication may be reproduced in a retrieval system, or transmitted in any form or by any means—electronic, mechanical, photocopying, recording, or otherwise—without the prior written permission of the publisher.

Unless otherwise noted, all scripture taken from the New King James Version®. Copyright © 1982 by Thomas Nelson. Used by permission. All rights reserved. | Scripture quotations marked (NRSV) are from the New Revised Standard Version Bible, copyright © 1989 National Council of the Churches of Christ in the United States of America. Used by permission. All rights reserved worldwide.

This manuscript has undergone viable editorial work and proofreading, yet human limitations may have resulted in minor grammatical or syntax-related errors remaining in the finished book. The understanding of the reader is requested in these cases. While precaution has been taken in the preparation of this book, the publisher and author assume no responsibility for errors or omissions, or for damages resulting from the use of the information contained herein.

This book is set in the typeface *Athelas* designed by Veronika Burian and Jose Scaglione.

Cover photography by Tawni Betts

Paperback ISBN: 979-8-3959-1482-8

A Publication of *Tall Pine Books*
119 E Center Street, Suite B4A | Warsaw, Indiana 46580
www.tallpinebooks.com

| 1 23 23 20 16 02 |

Published in the United States of America

UNPACKING A *TRADITIONAL* CHRISTMAS

---

25 SONGS *AND* STORIES
FOR THE SEASON

MARK HECHT & JANET LORD

The first person to place my tiny fingers on a piano was my Aunt Ruth, and my contributions to this book are dedicated to her. For 50 years she taught hundreds of children, including me, the great Sunday School songs like "Jesus Loves Me" and "This Little Light of Mine" as well as patiently guiding our stuttering efforts towards learning The Lord's Prayer. There are countless women in large and small churches who have done the same, nurturing the faith and creating memories. May their tribe continue.
—JANET LORD

I have been blessed with many wonderful role models over the course of my lifetime. I am grateful for the lessons I learned by listening to their stories and watching how they lived out their faith. The earliest and longest lasting influence was my grandmother, Agnes Miller. She lived what most would consider to be a "hard" life. But through it all exhibited faith in her Lord and love for her family. I would like to believe that her example has helped me to do the same. I dedicate this book to her memory.
—MARK HECHT

CONTENTS

Introduction 1

1. The Beginning of Christmas 5
2. Dear Santa... 11
3. Once Upon a Time 19
4. The Family Album 25
5. What's That Smell???? 31
6. Coal for Christmas 35
7. Plasticville Houses 41
8. Lights, Camera, Action 47
9. The Island of Misfit Toys 53
10. Bathrobes and Tinsel 59
11. Silly Sand 63
12. Sharing at Christmas 67
13. Window on Main Street 77
14. The Gift of Love 81
15. The Christmas Wreath 87
16. Making Christmas Just Right 91
17. Grandma's Ornament 97
18. Entering the Picture 103
19. Misplacing Jesus 107
20. Nativity Scenes 115
21. The Living Nativity 121
22. Are We There Yet? 127
23. Tapestry 137
24. Lullabies and Morning Praise 141
25. Why Worship Matters 151

Meet the Authors 159

INTRODUCTION

A NOTE FROM MARK:

THIRTY-FIVE YEARS OF ministry have afforded me countless opportunities to reflect upon the "true meaning of Christmas." Each new holiday season offers a chance to remember fondly the stories of my childhood as well as anticipate the new joy filled experiences God has in store for the present. What I have come to realize over the course of my life is that in many ways, Ecclesiastes had it correct:

> What has been will be again, what has been done will be done again; there is nothing new under the sun. (Ecclesiastes 1:9)

Agnes M. Pahro once penned that *"Christmas is tenderness for the past, courage for the present, hope for the future."* In a very real sense, Christmas is and always has been about reflecting back and looking ahead. The challenge, I believe, is to be certain to look in the proper place.

Did you ever stay up half the night on Christmas eve assembling a toy or bike? You quietly opened the box and carefully unpacked all the pieces only to realize the directions were missing. Perhaps the directions were inadvertently thrown away. Maybe the manufacturer forgot to include them. A project you expected to take fifteen minutes suddenly turned into an "all-nighter" accompanied by some less-than Christmas appropriate language! Regardless of whose fault it may be, more often than not, when we fail to follow the directions it takes longer to complete the task!

Each year, sometime in November or December, we make a decision to "unpack Christmas." We bring down the dusty plastic totes from the attic and bring up the musty cardboard boxes from the basement. They are opened and once again memories of Christmas's past spring forth. The collection of stories in this devotional are my attempt to "unpack Christmas." It is with great affection that I remember the people and places mentioned even as I anticipate what new joy will be experienced this holiday season. And I am able to do this because I take the time to "read the directions." Likewise, each of these accounts begins with scripture and ends with prayer, allowing God to provide direction as we work toward the celebration of Christ's birth.

A NOTE FROM JANET ABOUT THE RECORDINGS:

The link to the music for this book will take you to piano recordings that I've done over the past couple of years. These are far from professionally recorded or digitally enhanced. Many were recorded on my phone and played on my out-of-tune piano. All of them could be better. You will hear frantic page turning, perhaps a sigh or two, certainly some wrong notes, and almost certainly a train whistle or two. I hope that you'll be kind and gracious.

Like many Christmas blessings, God works with what is at hand. What I hope you hear *behind* those things is the heart with which I played them. These are some of my favorite arrangements from 50+ years of providing Christmas music in churches. Two years ago I put them together into a musical Advent calendar and found a way to share that through Facebook. When I unpack these pieces of music each year, see the notes that I've made in the margins, and play them again, they bring back memories of special people long gone and remembrances of the various churches where I've been privileged to offer music. My prayer is that while listening you may remember special people and times in your own life, and that by remembering you feel a sense of Christmas peace.

1
THE BEGINNING OF CHRISTMAS

But you, O Bethlehem of Ephrathah, who are one of the little clans of Judah, from you shall come forth for me one who is to rule in Israel, whose origin is from of old, from ancient days. Therefore, he shall give them up until the time when she who is in labor has brought forth; then the rest of his kindred shall return to the people of Israel. And he shall stand and feed his flock in the strength of the LORD, in the majesty of the name of the LORD his God. And they shall live secure, for now he shall be great to the ends of the earth; and he shall be the one of peace. (Micah 5:2-5)

WHEN DOES CHRISTMAS begin? And I don't just mean at what point on the church calendar do we officially move from the celebration of the Advent season to the joy of Christmas. When I was a child growing up in central Pennsylvania, I always knew when Christmas began. It was the moment on the day after Thanksgiving when Santa Clause parachuted from a plane onto the roof of the Sears and Roebuck Store at the Logan Valley Mall in Altoona. For some Christmas begins with the first batch of sugar cookies you take from the oven, or the first Christmas card you receive in the mail. To a previous generation it might have been when Bing Crosby and family aired their annual Christmas special, or the moment Burl Ives, as Sam the Snowman sang *Silver and Gold* on *Rudolph the Red Nosed Reindeer.*

In many ways, Christmas begins as we reflect back upon what has been with fondness and joy in our hearts, even as we participate once more in the hustle and bustle that is Christmas this year. We hang decorations on our trees that hung on the trees of our youth. We use cookie recipes passed down from Grandma. Whether we trim the tree three weeks before Christmas or on Christmas Eve, we likely do so because it's the way our parents did when we were children. All these events and so many more allow us the opportunity to celebrate the moment here and now even as they enable us to remember what once was with great fondness.

For each of us, Christmas begins at a slightly different moment. But what about from a scriptural perspective? When, in fact, does Christmas begin? Some might answer, it is the moment the angel appears to

Mary and tells her that she *"will conceive and bear a child"*. Others suggest the story begins when the angels announce to the shepherds *"For unto you is born this day in the city of David a Savior which is Christ the Lord"*.

But the real Christmas story begins much earlier; several hundred years earlier, in fact. One Old Testament prophecy after another promised a coming Savior, a Messiah who would redeem the people of God. The centerpiece of all the Christmas prophecies was written nearly six hundred years before Jesus' birth.

"For unto us a child is born, unto us a son is given: and the government shall be upon his shoulder: and his name shall be called Wonderful, Counsellor, The mighty God, The everlasting Father, The Prince of Peace" (Isaiah 9:6).

Like the other prophets under the guidance of the Holy Spirit he was able to see across the centuries and give us an amazingly accurate and all-encompassing picture of the Savior's birth. He promised it would be a miraculous event, unlike any the world had ever known. Isaiah, Micah and others offer words that were preparing the world for what was to come.

The problem is that two thousand years ago, and perhaps even more so this very day, humanity demonstrated an inability to look and listen, study, learn and try to understand that those messages from the Old Testament were and are part of the Christmas story. They were more than cute and entertaining coincidences to be acknowledged and taken lightly. No, in these words, hundreds of years before the birth of the Christ child, the story of Christmas began!

The truth is that Christmas has the ability to begin anew in our lives and world each and every year. We all stand in need of a Savior. We live in a sin sick world. Yet even in the darkest of days, it is possible for Christmas to bring good tidings of great joy.

It was the winter of 1863. The previous summer, this country had seen the horrors of Gettysburg, the bloodiest and deadliest single event in the history of our country. The Civil War was raging on and the world must have seemed to many as if it were coming apart. In the midst of it all, the poet Henry Wadsworth Longfellow penned one of his most famous poems: "Christmas Bells." A number of verses no longer appear on cards or in the carols we sing, but they are telling of the conditions of this land.

> Then from each black accursed mouth,
> the cannon thundered in the south,
> and with the sound the carols drowned
> of peace on earth good will to men.
>
> It was as if an earthquake rent
> the hearthstones of a continent,
> and made forlorn the households born,
> of peace on earth good will to men.
> And in despair I bowed my head,
> there is no peace on earth I said,

for hate is strong and mocks the song
of peace on earth good will to men.

Then on Christmas morning that year, Longfellow heard a single church bell ringing in the steeple of the town church. It wasn't much, but it was enough to give him hope.

Then pealed the bells more loud and deep,
God is not dead, nor doth he sleep,
The wrong, shall fail, the right prevail,
with peace on earth good will to men!

Consider how God uses Christmas to bring light to our lives. And as he does this, we are encouraged and emboldened to do the same for others. One bell ringing, one card sent to an elderly relative, one phone call made to a friend saddened by the loss of their loved one, one hour given to those less fortunate than oneself, or one prayer lifted to God on behalf of another. One little act, making all the difference in letting another know that God is here and that God loves and forgives us and that Jesus Christ is Lord.

When will Christmas begin for you this year? I pray the gift of the Christ Child is one you will cherish but also pass along to family and friend alike. Thanks be to God for a new beginning to Christmas this year and for our opportunity to share it with others.

Prayer: Redeeming God, enter our lives afresh this Advent season. Let Christmas not so much begin but continue as we reach out to others with Your love. May every bell remind us that Jesus came bringing peace on earth and good will to us all. Amen.

Musical Reflection: "I Heard the Bells on Christmas Day"

Scan the QR Code below to hear the Musical Reflection

2
DEAR SANTA...

Behold, the days come, saith the LORD, that I will perform that good thing which I have promised unto the house of Israel and to the house of Judah. In those days, and at that time, will I cause the Branch of righteousness to grow up unto David; and he shall execute judgment and righteousness in the land, In those days shall Judah be saved, and Jerusalem shall dwell safely: and this is the name wherewith she shall be called, The LORD our righteousness. (Jeremiah 33:14-16)

For what thanks can we render to God again for you, for all the joy wherewith we joy for your sakes before our God; Night and day praying exceedingly that we might see your face, and might perfect that which is lacking in your faith? Now God himself and our Father, and our Lord Jesus Christ, direct our way unto you. And the Lord make you to increase and abound in love one toward another, and toward all men, even as we do toward you: To the end he may stablish your hearts unblameable in holiness before God, even our Father, at the coming of our Lord Jesus Christ with all his saints. (1 Thessalonians 3:9-13)

"DEAR SANTA, I'VE been a very good boy this year, I did well in school, listened to my parents, and kept my room clean! And despite that little incident with the rock and my brother, I am very sorry, but I would point out that he is fully recovered. This year for Christmas I would like the following items..." The list would inevitably go on and on and eventually close with, "PS: there will be a plate of cookies and a glass of milk waiting for you by the tree. Sincerely, Mark Hecht"

The writing of the annual Christmas letter to Santa. Perhaps no other activity in the life of a young child took as much time and preparation as did this. I remember our letters had to be ready to hand to Santa's elves as they walked alongside him in the Christmas parade the day after Thanksgiving. So in order to be ready, we had to begin sometime in October to make sure we hadn't forgotten anything.

First, we would gather together the Penney's and

Sears catalogues, then newspaper advertisements from other stores. We then spent hours going over page after page of toys. Next we would check with our friends, to see what they wanted and what they were asking for. The entire process took days, and many hours of hard work. But that was alright because we knew Christmas was coming and this whole process only helped to add to that excitement.

I'll have you know that one Christmas Santa himself even called me on the phone several days before Christmas! I was shocked! Not only did Santa know my name and where I lived, but he also knew my phone number too! I still remember sitting in the kitchen when the phone rang and my father saying it was for me. I held the receiver to my ear and listened to Santa tell me that I was getting one gift early this year and that I should go to the front porch and pick it up. I quickly put down the phone, went to the door, and there on the porch sat a new train set for around our Christmas tree.

Some people say that Santa Claus doesn't have a place in Christmas. But I don't agree. St. Nicholas, Kris Kringle, Santa Claus, or whatever you call him, does indeed have his place, and while I don't think Santa should be parading down the aisles of our churches, I do think the spirit of Christmas, the spirit of giving and the joy of receiving is embodied in the old fellow.

Where we run into problems is when we allow Santa and parties and shopping to become the only things that are important this time of year. When we forget what in fact Christmas is really all about.

There is the story of the minister that was asked by his choir director, if he would pick up the sheet music for "How Great Thou Art" the next time he was in town. Well it just so happened that the following day he found himself at the local mall, so he went in a record store (it's an old story!) and asked the clerk, "Do you carry any religious sheet music?" The clerk who must have been in her teens thought for a moment and then said, "Some of the Christmas music might be religious!"

Likewise, some of what we do during the holiday season *might* be religious. This is what we need to remind ourselves during the season. In the midst of all the excitement and anticipation, we must remember that what we are really anticipating is the birth of one who came into the world to save it from itself.

Remember the prophecy from Jeremiah: "Behold the days are coming, says the Lord, when I will fulfill the promise I made to the house of Israel and the house of Judah."

Excitement and expectation are what it's all about! Hopefully we realize that this should be our attitude each and every day of the year, but we should be especially attuned to it during this season.

The term Advent means waiting for the coming of our Lord; anticipating something that has not yet occurred! Probably the biggest complaint of believers, other than the issue of Christmas losing its religious significance is that, "Christmas never seems to be as exciting as it should be." I anticipate and anticipate and once the day arrives, I think to myself, "Big deal, so what, I guess I'll just wait until next year." With Christmas the expectation is often greater than the actual event.

I would be lying if I didn't admit that I am often times one of the people with that very attitude. But recently I have been thinking, whose fault is it that this occurs? In his letter to the Thessalonians, Paul writes to tell them that he continues to pray with thanksgiving to God for them even though they are still lacking faith. And while he could have left it at that, he goes on to say *"Now may our God and Father Himself and Jesus our Lord direct our way to you. And may the Lord cause you to increase and abound in love for one another and for all, just as we also do for you."*

Paul sees something good and exciting and isn't afraid to mess it up by asking for even more. He could have been content to say to the church, "You guys are just fine! We'll pray for you and see you soon!" But he doesn't! He wants things to be even greater, and we can sense the excitement and anticipation in his voice as he continues *"so that God may establish your hearts unblameable in holiness before our God and Father the coming of our Lord Jesus with all His saints."*

And so as Paul awaits his meeting with the church in Thessalonica, and the joy that it will bring to all involved, we await the coming (the advent) of our savior and all the joy and excitement that it can bring.

If Christmas disappoints us, we have no one to blame but ourselves. This is indeed a season of Joy! We remember that God loved us enough to come into the world, and if we cannot anxiously look forward to celebrating that fact, we are a people without hope, and more importantly, we are not acting like Christians.

An old pioneer traveled westward across the Great Plains until he came to an abrupt halt at the edge of the Grand Canyon. He gawked at the sight before him; a vast chasm one mile down, eighteen miles across and more than a hundred miles long. He gasped, "Something must have happened here!" A visitor to our world at Christmas time, seeing lights decorations, trees, parades, festivities, and even religious services would also probably say, "Something must have happened here!" Indeed, something did happen. God came to our world on the first Christmas.

Excitement, anticipation, and joy. They are all part of the season. May the coming days be filled with that excitement and joy for one and all. Christ is coming once again, wait and celebrate!

Prayer: God of anticipation, light our path this Advent season so that we see Your light beaming out in even the darkest places. Let those lights guide us to the manger, and to Your great presence with us. Amen.

Musical Reflection: "Come, Thou Long-Expected Jesus"

Scan the QR Code below to hear the Musical Reflection

3
ONCE UPON A TIME

And when they were come into the house, they saw the young child with Mary his mother, and fell down, and worshipped him: and when they had opened their treasures, they presented unto him gifts; gold, and frankincense and myrrh. (Matthew 2:11)

"ONCE UPON A time Red Riding Hood was on her way to....the homes of the three little pigs...who helped Cinderella prepare for the ball.... and Jack climb the giant beanstalk...when just then, the wicked witch frightened Hansel and Gretel... as the cow jumped over the moon...and they all lived happily ever after."

"What kind of story is that?!" you might be thinking. Well, let me explain. When our son Joshua was two years old, he had a very large book of stories and nursery rhymes that he loved for us to read to him. The only problem was that he was often impatient when it came to listening to the entire story. I would begin on page one, and he would turn to 44, then 65, then 88 and 102. In a matter of minutes, we made our way to the end of the book, but never once heard or experienced an entire story. Now to his two-year-old ears, heart and mind, Joshua believed he had in fact heard it all, yet nothing could be further from the truth.

By not taking the time to look at the whole story, so very much was missed along the way. In similar fashion, I believe we make a great mistake and do ourselves and our God a great disservice when we jump right from that first Christmas with an unwelcome baby lying in a manger stall, visited by lowly shepherds and Magi from the east...directly to the present day, where we await all the expensive and high-tech toys and gifts under our trees on Christmas morning. It is like turning the pages of my son's story book all those years ago and missing so very much of what takes place in between.

It is important to understand that the Christmas story does not end with wisemen delivering gifts of gold, frankincense and myrrh. The deaf and blind writer, Helen Keller, who could not see with her eyes but saw things very clearly with her heart, once put it this way:

> "The legend tells that when Jesus was born the sun danced in the sky, the aged trees

straightened themselves and put on leaves and sent forth the fragrance of blossoms once more. These are the symbols of what takes place in our hearts when the Christ child is born anew each year. Blessed by the Christmas sunshine, our natures, perhaps long leafless, bring forth new love, new kindness, new mercy, new compassion. As the birth of Jesus was the beginning of the Christian life, so the unselfish joy at Christmas shall start the spirit that is to rule the new year."

The story of Christmas, the joy of this season, and the meaning and spirit of the holiday comes to us 2000 plus years later, not by skipping over time but by journeying through it!

It was the precious gift of the prince of peace, a Messiah willing to give his very life to save those he loved, that inspired a young man named Nicholas in early 4th century Asia Minor to share with and care for others in need. St Nicholas gave all he ever had away to help others because the Christ child was born anew in his life.

As the story made its way through the years, it was a spirit of caring and compassion that touched the heart of an otherwise selfish King Henry III of England in 1248, as he established the custom of giving food to the needy for the holiday. And in doing so the Christ Child was born anew in the life of the people.

In 1818 assistant priest Father Joseph Mohr was preparing for the Christmas service in the church of St. Nicholas, high in the alps, distressed over the fact that the church's organ was not working when he was asked to go to the house of a poor family to bless a newborn baby. Walking home through the snow, the spirit of Christmas was at work in his heart as he thought about the first Christmas and was inspired to write the words of a carol.

He quickly took them to his musician friend Franz Gruber who wrote the music in an hour. As Mohr played his guitar, he and Gruber and two other singers sang the new carol for the first time that Christmas.

> "Silent night, holy night, all is calm, all is bright round yon virgin mother and child; holy infant so tender and mild, sleep in heavenly peace, sleep in heavenly peace."

And as the Christ Child was born anew in lives that year a carol was born that has shared the story for over 200 years!

In 1843 the spirit of Christmas again was shared as Charles Dickens penned the words to "A Christmas Carol". The story of the transformation that takes place in the life of one Ebenezer Scrooge is a message of repentance and hope. Again, mindful of the true meaning of the holiday, we rejoice that God sent us salvation, that blessed Christmas morn.

And then there are the stories of individual families that have been passed down over the decades to help us remember why we celebrate. Even in this digital world in which we live, we have been known to pull out the old 8-millimeter home movies and VHS tapes and watch our parents' first Christmas together, the toys we received as children, and fondly remember those no longer with us. And in doing so we are allowing the spirit of joy and giving, love and sharing that is Christmas to pass through our lives once more.

There is a church in Bethlehem, built over a cave where Christian legend has it that Jesus spent his first night in this world. Bethlehem actually means "house of bread". If you have the time and the money you can go to Bethlehem and see it for yourself. But you don't need to go to Bethlehem to receive its blessings and benefits. Bethlehem comes to us! In the celebration of a baby's birth, Christ "the living Bread which came down from heaven" comes to us to feed us, to give us His life, to make our hearts His manger.

He comes to us through the ages, to our here and now, the same way he did that holy night two thousand years ago. He comes to us through the centuries in the stories of Saints, the history of family and the blessings of friends.

The holy child of Bethlehem greets us once again this year! The pages of the storybook that is the life of God's people continue to turn. This season celebrate the fact that we are a part of that story. And as the pages of that book turn, relish each one, share each new story, and rejoice that Christmas is coming once more. And because of this....WE CAN ALL LIVE HAPPILY EVER AFTER.

> **Prayer:** *"O come, Thou Dayspring, come and cheer our spirits by Thine advent here;*
>
> *Disperse the gloomy clouds of night and death's dark shadows put to flight.*
>
> *Rejoice! Rejoice! Emmanuel shall come to thee, O Israel"* (Latin hymn, v.4; #162 <u>Our Great Redeemer's Praise</u>)
>
> **Musical Reflecton:** O Come, O Come, Emmanuel

Scan the QR Code below to hear the Musical Reflection

4
THE FAMILY ALBUM

An account of the genealogy of Jesus the Messiah, the son of David, the son of Abraham. (Matthew 1:1-17)

ABRAHAM WAS THE father of Isaac, and Isaac the father of Jacob, and Jacob the father of Judah and his brothers, and Judah the father of Perez and Zerah by Tamar, and Perez the father of Hezron, and Hezron the father of Aram, and Aram the father of Aminadab, and Aminadab the father of Nahshon, and Nahshon the father of Salmon, and Salmon the father of Boaz by Rahab, and Boaz the father of Obed by Ruth, and Obed the father of Jesse, and Jesse the father of King David.

And David was the father of Solomon by the wife of Uriah, and Solomon the father of Rehoboam, and Rehoboam the father of Abijah, and Abijah the father of Asaph, and Asaph the father of Jehoshaphat, and Jehoshaphat the father of Joram, and Joram the father of Uzziah, and Uzziah the father of Jotham, and Jotham the father of Ahaz, and Ahaz the father of Hezekiah, and Hezekiah the father of Manasseh, and Manasseh the father of Amos, and Amos the father of Josiah, and Josiah the father of Jechoniah and his brothers, at the time of the deportation to Babylon.

And after the deportation to Babylon: Jechoniah was the father of Salathiel, and Salathiel the father of Zerubbabel, and Zerubbabel the father of Abiud, and Abiud the father of Eliakim, and Eliakim the father of Azor, and Azor the father of Zadok, and Zadok the father of Achim, and Achim the father of Eliud, and Eliud the father of Eleazar, and Eleazar the father of Matthan, and Matthan the father of Jacob, and Jacob the father of Joseph the husband of Mary, of whom Jesus was born, who is called the Messiah.

So all the generations from Abraham to David are fourteen generations; and from David to the deportation to Babylon, fourteen generations; and from the deportation to Babylon to the Messiah, fourteen generations.

Why the genealogy of Jesus, today? Why go to the trouble of reading a list of names, some familiar, others not? What could possibly be so important about these individuals that they warrant special time and remembrance during our Christmas celebration? Does it really matter what came before Christ? Since Jesus Christ came into the world hasn't everything been changed? What came before is no longer important. Sure it might be worthy of a footnote in the great book of history. But worth spending time and energy studying and attempting to understand, I don't think so.

If that is the attitude that we bring to this scripture lesson and in general to our study of and understanding of the Bible and its story, then we are truly a people without hope. For if we fail to look beyond the events of that stable in Bethlehem to those things and peoples that preceded Christ's coming into the world we miss the point as to why he came, and why he had do what he did on Calvary's cross when he died that we might live.

By naming but a few of those individuals who preceded Christ's coming into the world, and linking his life to theirs, Matthew displays a continuity and order of God's purpose among God's people. We hear the name of Abraham, the patriarch of the faith and remember the covenant that God made with him. We see the name of David and remember the establishing of a kingdom of God's people. Other names remind us of the exile into Babylon, and all ultimately led up to the birth of Jesus Christ.

What Matthew has done in just a few lines is to give us a glimpse of the individuals that helped shape the people of God; who in effect made the people of Jesus' day who they were.

Let me tell you briefly about my great-great-great-great-great-grandmother. Her name was Maria Appolonia "Abigail" Hartman Rice. She was born in

Württemberg, Germany in 1742 and immigrated to America with her family as a child to the Philadelphia area. Abigail married as a teen and over the next two and half decades gave birth to twenty-two children. During the Revolutionary War Abigail worked as a nurse through the winter of 1777-78 at Valley Forge helping to care for the sick and dying troops of George Washington. Family records indicate that while in this service Abigail contracted typhoid fever, which eventually brought about her own death. Seventeen of her twenty-two children, including my grandmother's great-great grandfather John Rice, her eldest son, attended her funeral.

I cannot help but think how there must be so many individuals who whose very lives and stories have been forgotten; persons who gave their all for their fellow men and women in this life and whose lives are directly related to our own.

Before you say it is too much trouble to remember or even care about those who came before, think about your own family. Every one of us had two parents, four grandparents, 8 great-grandparents, 16 great-great grandparents, 32 great-great-great grandparents. And if you remove just one of those individuals, just one, from that family tree, you are not here today! Every single one of those people played an essential part in literally making you who you are.

And there have been still others, I am sure, including step-parents or aunts and uncles, or friends of the family who have indirectly influenced you over your lifetime, and helped to make you what you are as well.

What better time of year to recognize and remember the importance of family and history and how it shapes who we are than right now at Christmas time? I was thinking the other day about how when the holidays rolled around each year we would pull out the old photo albums or get out the home movies and reminisce about past Christmases. As a matter of fact, I was going through some old photo albums several weeks ago and for the first time noticed that a majority of all the pictures my family had taken and saved were in fact from previous Christmases. What is it about Christmas that causes us to remember?

I also remember how my grandmother and I would go through the family album. The faces were vaguely familiar to me but she was able to remember something about many of the people and share it with me. "This was your great uncle so and so; he used to do this or that." Or, "This was Mrs. Jones, she lived next door. Every year at Christmas time she would bring over plates of cookies to your grandparents."

Christmas was and is a time for celebrating friends and family. And it is also a time to remember who we are and who was responsible for bringing us to where we are today. Not all the memories that come to mind this time of year are easy ones, however. Because with the joy of celebrating with friends and family often times comes the reminders of those who are no longer with us. But don't be afraid to remember. And don't be afraid to share your memories with others. Who you are is directly related to those individuals you may miss or think about. Celebrate this season of love by remembering the love that has been shared with you.

> **Prayer:** Creating God, You have seen all of our days before we are even born. You have watched over generations before us and will guard those who come after us. Help us to faithfully walk according to your Word and fulfill our place in Your great plan. Amen.

Musical Reflection: "What Child is This?"

Scan the QR Code below to hear the Musical Reflection

5
WHAT'S THAT SMELL????

(BY JANET LORD)

> But thanks be to God, who in Christ always leads us in triumphal procession and through us spreads in every place the fragrance that comes from knowing him. For we are the aroma of Christ to God among those who are being saved and among those who are perishing. (2 Corinthians 2:14,15 NSRV)

SOMETIME IN DECEMBER when I was a child there would come a Saturday that began with sounds of heavy objects being banged against the doorframe as they were carried into the house. This was followed by hammering and louder than usual "discussions" between my parents. At this point I was usually too curious to stay in bed, but also excited because I knew what was happening: my parents were creating magic! At the end of all of the loud hammering noise would come the much more pleasant, gentle sound of the Lionel train making its way around the 4 x 8 platform that would eventually hold our Christmas tree and presents!

Trains, in themselves, are no strangers to our family. The Norfolk/Southern freight line rumbles through at least 15 times a day on the tracks that are literally across the street from our house, right by a crossing. For as long as I can remember trains and whistles have provided the background noise of my life. I learned to count by sitting on the front porch with my Dad and counting the cars as they went by. The sound of the *real* trains is neither pleasant nor gentle. But the soothing clickety-clack of the train under the Christmas tree? That noise was reassuring and with it came the promise of even better things.

More magical than even the sound, though, was the smell. If you grew up in the 50s or 60s you know what I mean. It was a combination of machine oil, electric sparks and ozone. If Yankee Candle was able to somehow capture it they would label it "Boomer Childhood Christmas". That smell, too, carried the promise of even better things to come.

Advent is just such a season. It's a special combination of familiar sights, sounds, and smells that both take us back to simpler times but also remind us that the gift that the Christ Child brings offers forgiveness, reconciliation, and new life.

As you unwrap those special memories this Advent season, allow space for the things yet unseen.

Prayer: Nurturing God, keep us mindful of your promises as we make our way through this special season. You are the God who keeps His promises. Remind us that the best is yet to come! Amen.

Musical Reflection: "Carol Medley"

Scan the QR Code below to hear the Musical Reflection

6
COAL FOR CHRISTMAS

For I was an hungered, and ye gave me meat: I was thirsty, and ye gave me drink: I was a stranger, and ye took me in: Naked, and ye clothed me: I was sick, and ye visited me: I was in prison, and ye came unto me. Then shall the righteous answer him, saying, Lord, when saw we thee an hungered, and fed thee? or thirsty, and gave thee drink? When saw we thee a stranger, and took thee in? or naked, and clothed thee? Or when saw we thee sick, or in prison, and came unto thee? And the King shall answer and say unto them, Verily I say unto you, Inasmuch as ye have done it unto one of the least of these my brethren, ye have done it unto me. (Matthew 25:35-40)

WHEN I WAS a young child growing up in the Central Pennsylvania town of Duncansville, my grandmother lived three blocks away from our house in a small upstairs apartment. Grandma didn't have much in the way of worldly possessions but I can always remember helping her to decorate that little two room apartment each holiday. We would go to the closet and pull the clear plastic tree off the shelf, add little gum ball candies all over it and place it on her small table in the kitchen.

Then we would set up an aluminum Christmas tree (it was the late 1960's after all!) in a corner of her liying room by her tiny Hammond organ where we would play Christmas carols and sing.

That was really about all, except, before the boxes that held the decorations were returned to the top shelf of the closet, Grandma would pull out a piece of coal and place it on the three tiered book case that held all her family pictures. And there it would sit for the entire month of December.

I remember asking her what it was for and she would simply say, "To help me remember." Remember what? She would always refuse to say. Every little boy and girl knows that children who end up on the naughty list also end up with a lump of coal in their stockings on Christmas morning. Surely Grandma was not trying to frighten the grandchildren into improving their behaviors. She was a gentle soul and that thought would truthfully never have crossed her mind. What could it be that she needed to remember?

The years passed and Grandma came and lived

with us for a little while and then on to a nursing home for the last years of her life. Still, each Christmas, if no other decoration went up, you could count on the lump of coal.

It was a year or so before her death and I was visiting with her at the home and asked if she would please explain the piece of coal. Thankfully, she finally agreed.

It was 1908. My grandmother Agnes would have been five years old at the time and her little brother Bill just three. Both children had been very sick that year, so much so that the doctor's bills almost sent my great grandparents Annie and Asbury to the poor house. Times were tough, and although the children's health was starting to improve the long cold winter lay ahead and Asbury's job for the Pennsylvania Railroad barely brought home enough to keep the house.

Christmas that year would be particularly difficult. There were to be no toys or gifts of any kind under the tree. You might assume the coal was a reminder of harder times when life was tough. Nothing could be further from the truth.

For as hard as things were that winter of 1908 there was also a blessing that came to my Grandma's family from a most unexpected source. In that same small town lived a curmudgeonly retired schoolteacher named Mr. Speck or "Daddy Speck", as everyone referred to him.

"Daddy Speck" didn't have any family. He had

a long and well-earned reputation as a stern "old school" educator who carried a large stick and wore a pair of wire rimmed glasses that clipped to the bridge of his nose. I was told that children in town both feared and loved this gruff old soul.

Well, it seems that "Daddy Speck" was also a neighbor of my great grandparents and knew of their difficulties. His concern was so great that on Christmas Eve he had delivered enough coal to heat the house for the entire winter. My great grandfather tried to thank him but he simply replied, "No need."

They attempted to give him something in return and again he refused. Daddy Speck's reply, "Didn't seem right....children cold at Christmas" and left.

And that Christmas morning, my Grandma said while she went to sleep in a cold house, she awakened in a warm home. Her family never forgot the generosity and care of Daddy Speck and Grandma said she kept that piece of coal to remind her to do whatever she could whenever she could to help others when they were in need.

A lump of coal might seem a lousy gift to many a child today. But one Christmas over a hundred years ago, a lump of coal was a symbol of God's love.

> **Prayer:** Providing God, thank you for using seemingly insignificant objects like a lump of coal to remind us of your great love and care for us. Help us to be mindful of the

needs of others and quick to respond. Amen.

Musical Reflection: "In The Bleak Midwinter"

Scan the QR Code below to hear the Musical Reflection

7
PLASTICVILLE HOUSES

Now all this was done, that it might be fulfilled which was spoken of the Lord by the prophet, saying, Behold, a virgin shall be with child, and shall bring forth a son, and they shall call his name Emmanuel, which being interpreted is, God with us. (Matthew 1:22-23)

SEVERAL YEARS AGO, my brother was clearing some items out of his home and offered me a box filled with Plasticville houses that were once placed under the tree each Christmas in our home when we were growing up. Even before I opened it, I knew exactly what I would find.

- 2-story beige house with carport on the side
- Yellow ranch style home
- White church with grey roof and tiny bell in the steeple that rang when you shook it
- Diner

- Red school house
- Ice cream stand
- 5-and-10 cent store
- Post office
- Two cape cod cottages one with red roof and one with gray

And sure enough, they were all there. Every year these same structures would surround the tree in our home on 6th Avenue in Duncansville. When I watch the old home movies I can still see them each in their proper place alongside the Lionel HO gauge train that circled the entire display. I was so happy to have those houses again. In fact, we keep several of them out year-round now on a shelf in our family room.

A few years after we were gifted with these houses, my father-in-law offered our family the O Gauge train set that was his, as a child. He had the entire train restored a few years prior and it had returned under the tree in his home ever since. We keep that locomotive and cars in a case on our mantel as well.

Why is that we keep these symbols of the holiday out in our home year-round? Years ago, I encouraged the congregation I was serving at the time to keep a nativity scene out at home year-round to remind us that Jesus came into our world and lives not just for a moment in time that we remember and celebrate on December 24th and 25th but rather, to be with us each and every day of our life.

Now consider those Plasticville houses once

more. What is required to get each of those Plasticville homes in just that right place and position each of the little figures carefully in front of each building? Additionally, what must one do to get the train carefully placed on the track and ready to go? Any child of the 60's knows the answer. In order to make it all work and look "just right" you need to get down on your hands and knees, lower your head to eye level with the houses and track and make certain everything is exactly where it needs to be. Otherwise, it doesn't work or at least it doesn't work properly.

Isn't this precisely what God has done in Jesus Christ at Christmas? God has gotten right down with us. He has come down to our level to see things the way we see them, in an effort to make it all work; to fix things. And because He is in our life amazing things are possible. That is what we celebrate in this season. God with us: Emmanuel.

The pastor in my home church while I was growing up I believe was a lifelong Methodist. But he had attended college at a Moravian school in Eastern Pennsylvania. While there he learned of and grew to appreciate the Christmas traditions of the Moravians. When he came to serve our church in Duncansville, he brought along his appreciation for these traditions and over time several were incorporated into the seasonal worship of that church. I wouldn't be surprised if some were still being used 50 years later.

One of these traditions involved celebrating the

"Morning Star". In Moravian churches and homes a large multi-pointed star hangs from the ceiling of the Sanctuary, filling the darkness with light. This is the "Morning Star", not the star of Bethlehem but the "Morning Star."

The star reminds us of God, who caused the light to shine out of darkness and of the light which is the life of humanity. It reminds us of the promise of Abraham that his descendants would be more numerous than the stars and also points to Jesus, who said, "I am the bright and Morning Star." It is the star of promise, the star of fulfillment, and the star of hope.

On Christmas Eve a child soprano soloist was chosen to lead a song and response with the congregation. "Morning Star, O cheering sight; ere thou camest how dark earth's night! Jesus, mine, in me shine; fill my heart with light divine."

So many of the symbols of the season are meant to remind us of the ways in which God enters into our broken world and in doing seeks to make things right. Take time this season to watch for the ways in which God is reaching out to make your life whole and fill your heart with "light divine."

> **Prayer:** God of Eternal Light, shine Your light again into the dark places of our lives. Thank for the gift of Jesus, who came to walk among us on our level to point the way to Your all-encompassing love. Amen.

Musical Reflection: "Still, Still, Still"

Scan the QR Code below to hear the Musical Reflection

8
LIGHTS, CAMERA, ACTION

The people that walked in darkness have seen a great light: they that dwell in the land of the shadow of death, upon them hath the light shined. For unto us a child is born, unto us a son is given: and the government shall be upon his shoulder: and his name shall be called Wonderful, Counsellor, The mighty God, The everlasting Father, The Prince of Peace. Of the increase of his government and peace there shall be no end, upon the throne of David, and upon his kingdom, to order it, and to establish it with judgment and with justice from henceforth even forever. The zeal of the LORD of hosts will perform this. (Isaiah 9:2, 6-7)

IF YOU GREW up in the 60's or 70's you most certainly remember your father's 8mm camera. The following scene was played out time and time again in our home. Dad pulled out the camera and began to record my brother and me. "OK boys look at the camera. Now wave. OK, stop looking at the camera and DO something!" Every home movie that we retrieve from cardboard boxes on the shelf in the hallway closet to watch during the holiday season follows the exact same script; scene after scene of two smiling brothers, waving and mouthing to the unseen person behind the camera, "What do you want us to do now?"

Every Christmas morning of my childhood was the same. Dad would stand outside our bedroom door with camera in hand as we awakened and stumbled down the hall to the living room. Christmas morning was special. And my father didn't want to miss anything. So, you could be certain that attached to the 8mm camera was the two-foot-long bar that I swear weighed a ton. And affixed to either end of that bar were lights! By lights I do not mean normal 60 watt bulbs. No, I remember them as each being approximately 10,000 watts! I have always assumed these were the same lights used on airport landing strips to direct planes at night!

Every year two little boys attempted to wipe the sleep from their eyes, while sitting under a Christmas tree opening presents, as those high intensity spotlights were turned on. The lights burned so brightly that we were always squinting as we turned towards the camera. I can still hear my father's voice calling out from somewhere "out there" behind the lights.

We could never see him. We only heard his voice directing us, "Show us what you got!" And we would respond by holding up the toy from Santa or the new sweater from Grandma.

Of course, lights and Christmas go together. During the holidays our homes and church sanctuaries are decorated with strings of lights. Some families still spend time driving through neighborhoods to gaze at the beautiful light displays neighbors have taken the time to arrange. The high point of worship this season is that moment when we sit or stand with candles in hand as we sing Silent Night. Light is indeed a significant part of the holiday.

Consider what Christmas would be like without lights. Would it be the same without the neighborhood displays? If there were no twinkling lights on the trees in our homes, would the tradition of bringing a dead evergreen into our living rooms be nearly as inviting and attractive? Would the mood of worship services be different without light in our sanctuaries?

What if we attempted to celebrate this December without the one true light of the world, the light of Christ? Would we be able to find the same joy, excitement and warmth in this season merely by wrapping gifts, decorating trees and attending parties even if Jesus had never come to earth?

There's a verse in a poem by M.R. DeHaan, entitled *Can This Be Christmas* that speaks to this point.

In countless homes the candles burning,
In countless hearts expectant yearning
For gifts and presents, food and fun,
And laughter till the day is done.
But not a tear of grief or sorrow.
For him so poor He had to borrow
A crib, a colt, a boat, a bed.
Where He could lay His weary head.
I'm tired of all this empty celebration,
Of feasting, drinking, recreation;
I'll go instead to Calvary.
And there I'll kneel with those who know
The meaning of that manger low,
And find the Christ- This Christmas.

The prophet Isaiah got it right. *The people that walked in darkness have seen a great light: they that dwell in the land of the shadow of death, upon them hath the light shined.* During this season the bright light of Christ shines into our world and lives. It has the ability to stop us right where we are, causing us to stare in awe and wonder. It shines on us because a God of love stands behind it, watching over us because of his love for us. How we choose to act in the light, however, is up to us. Do we listen to the voice calling out of the light to come to him? Do we show him "what we got" and who we really are? Or do we continue to go about our daily lives ignoring his presence and think only of ourselves?

Note and take to heart the closing lines of *Can This Be Christmas;*

> I leap by faith across the years
> To that great day when He appears
> The second time, to rule and reign,
> To end all sorrow, death and pain.
> In endless bliss we then shall dwell
> With Him who saved our souls from hell,
> And worship Christ- not Christmas!

Prayer: God of Fulfilled Promises, help us to always place our expectations in Your loving hands. Remind us that You are constantly setting the scene for what is to come. May we look for your coming again with joyful anticipation. Amen.

Musical Reflection: "For Unto Us a Child is Born"

Scan the QR Code below to hear the Musical Reflection

9

THE ISLAND OF MISFIT TOYS

And it came to pass, that, when Elisabeth heard the salutation of Mary, the babe leaped in her womb; and Elisabeth was filled with the Holy Ghost: And she spake out with a loud voice, and said, Blessed art thou among women, and blessed is the fruit of thy womb. And whence is this to me, that the mother of my Lord should come to me? For, lo, as soon as the voice of thy salutation sounded in mine ears, the babe leaped in my womb for joy. And blessed is she that believed: for there shall be a performance of those things which were told her from the Lord. And Mary said, "My soul doth magnify the Lord, And my spirit hath rejoiced in God my Savior. For he hath regarded the low estate of his handmaiden: for, behold, from henceforth all generations shall call me blessed. For he that is mighty hath done to me great things; and holy is his name." (Luke 1:41-49)

OF ALL THE stop-motion animation Christmas specials from my youth, *Rudolph the Red-Nosed Reindeer* has always been my favorite. It was first broadcast the year I was born so I literally grew up assuming this was an expected part of each holiday season. But beyond "tradition" what is it about this show that speaks to my heart each time I view it? I have given much thought to this question and have concluded that it has everything to do with.... MISFITS!

Whether we like to admit it or not, there are plenty of times in life when we feel like a misfit or at the very least, as though we simply don't belong. The story of Rudolph is meant to remind the viewer that there is, in fact, room and a place for the "misfits."

The star of course is Rudolph. Rudolph is considered a misfit due to the fact that he was born with a nose that glowed. He was different and the other reindeer made fun of him. Even his father told him to "turn that nose down!" All of the teasing leads Rudolph to take off into the wilderness just as a big storm is moving in. He meets up with Hermey the elf (another misfit) who wanted to be a dentist. Together they decide to leave the teasing behind and run away. In the course of their adventures they encounter the "Abominable Snow Monster" or Bumble. They escape and meet Yukon Cornelius the explorer. And end up on the island of Misfit toys. Rudolph's shiny nose saves Christmas and the misfits themselves tell Santa about the island of misfit toys.

This story touches our heart, because it reminds us that there is a place for the misfit. It tells a story of determined individuals who make a difference in the world for good. Even the Abominable Snow Monster, the Bumble, is rehabilitated and can put the star on the Christmas tree. I believe there is a message of hope in this tale. The message is that "I have a purpose and there is something I can contribute."

Some might claim that Jesus, in fact, came into the world for "The Misfits"! And who are "The Misfits"? We are! Each one of us is valuable to God. Each of us has a place in God's plan.

Consider the scripture from Luke. The lead characters are a young peasant girl, engaged to be married and a humble carpenter from Nazareth. As if their meager backgrounds were not enough, Mary's pregnancy out of wedlock would certainly make these two poster children for the island of misfits.

The amazing thing is; however, God uses misfits! If you look at the scripture you see that Mary has been told that she is the one to bear the Son of God. The scriptures explain it this way; *So all this was done that it might be fulfilled which was spoken by the Lord through the prophet, saying: "Behold, the virgin shall be with child, and bear a Son, and they shall call His name Immanuel," which is translated, "God with us." (Matthew 1:22-23)*

God is going to use Mary in an amazing way. But look at her background. Not exactly what one might expect of the woman chosen to bear the Son of God. Clearly, she is worthy of the title "misfit." But she does have something that makes all the difference. She believes!

And God looks into the heart of this "misfit" and shares, "This is my will for your life," and she responds with confidence, "Let it be."

Have you ever felt like a "misfit?"

Let me take you back to the island once more. Remember all those toys on that island. When it came to some of the toys it was obvious what made them "misfits". A train with square wheels and a bird that swims are obvious. But then there is a Jack-in-the-Box named Charlie and a doll whose "misfittedness" is never explained. Could it be that some of the things that make us different are on the outside and some things, like feelings, are on the inside?

Sometimes the misfit feeling is known only to us and we share it with no one. The thing is that those feelings have a way of making their way to the surface during the holiday season, turning potentially joyful holidays into "Blue Christmases" with little or no warning.

If you ever find yourself feeling like this, remember you matter to God. He sent his Son to redeem you and you have a place in God's plan. You are not forgotten. Remember the toys. They were not forgotten either. Mary's story reminds us that in God's plan there is something for all. There is most certainly a place for the misfit. In God's plan it is those who are hurting, marginalized, or poor that God picks up and uses for His glory.

> **Prayer:** Thank you for being the God Who Notices, who sees us when we find it hard to really see ourselves, who calls us out of our dark corners to walk with You in the Light of Christ. Help us to notice, as well, those around us who feel abandoned, overlooked, or forgotten. May Your light shine brightly through us. Amen.

Musical Reflection: "All is Well"

Scan the QR Code below to hear the Musical Reflection

10
BATHROBES AND TINSEL

(BY JANET LORD)

> Then little children were being brought to him in order that he might lay his hands on them and pray. The disciples spoke sternly to those who brought them; but Jesus said, "Let the children come to me, and do not stop them; for it is to such as these that the kingdom of heaven belongs." (Matthew 19: 13-14 NSRV)

AT SOME POINT in your life, have you experienced any of the following?

- Received a gift that you weren't thrilled with but also thought that the container would make a great prop for a Wise Man to carry?
- Purchased a not-so-attractive bathrobe for a male relative with the primary intent being to re-purpose it in a few years into a shepherd's robe?
- Experimented with various types of glue to

find the best adhesive for cotton balls on cardboard?
- Purchased bulk packs of white socks to transform toddlers' forearms into sheep legs?
- Spent more than 10 minutes evaluating tinsel for its color, heft and flexibility?
- Stored any or all of these things in a plastic tote in an inconvenient corner of a storage room at a church?

If so, while not entitled to legal representation or compensation, you just might be a Children's Christmas Program Director.

I'm currently in recovery from just such a condition, but for many years the intricacies of the Christmas Program occupied a large part of my thoughts from mid-August until the second week of December. I would agonize over choosing the "right" musical (the Biblical story need to be clearly stated), the casting (fortunately I usually had some eager over-achievers), the costumes, learning the songs, allowing for snow days, repeating my mantra of "No live animals; no live babies", and enlisting the help of sometimes reluctant parents.

One memorable year, the only available boy for a central role with lots of lines was my own son. There was no nepotism at play here. As task-oriented as I am, my son is, well, not. We would rehearse lines endlessly at home but at rehearsals he gave no indication that he had ever heard them before. As the day drew near I recruited a prompter to be sequestered behind a Christmas tree and hoped for the best. The program began and I sat in astonishment as my son not only spoke his lines like a miniature Tom Hanks but also prompted *other* kids suddenly taken by stage fright. It was a Christmas miracle!

Why did I put myself through this? Like most Christmas traditions, I thought it was expected of me. But beyond that, a part of me wanted to give these children two things: a good grounding in the real Christmas story, and some good memories to carry them through whatever life threw their way.

One of the aforementioned over-achievers could always be counted on to learn the songs, know his lines, and always show up for rehearsals. He had a creative streak, but always channeled it to make things better for everyone. One year, he was cast as Reuben the Shepherd Boy. He got to wear what was possibly the oldest and certainly the most tattered of the Shepherd Wardrobe Collection, but it fit him well. We added one of our trademark aluminum shepherd crooks (readily available at the First Century Bethlehem Alcoa Outlet) and he was ready to go. The highlight of the musical that year was a Dixieland rendition of the shepherds rejoicing on the hillside. "Reuben" knew all of the words and had sung it perfectly for weeks. The day of the program, however, he was accompanied by the Holy Spirit that led him to add dance moves worthy of Fred Astaire. It was another beautiful Christmas moment.

Around 30 years later, I carried that tattered robe and aluminum crook (having retrieved them from the storage closet) with me as I walked with "Reuben" to the kneeler at Annual Conference when he was ordained. That was a Holy Moment, not just for him but for me as I received a sense of reassurance that all of the rehearsals, planning, and frustrations had made a difference not just for him but for all of the children...and for their parents...and for me. Jesus comes for us all, sometimes in imperfect ways, often when we least expect it.

> **Prayer:** God of the Manger, help us not to overlook ordinary things and ordinary people as we journey towards Christmas, because that is precisely where Your miracles are hidden. Amen.

Musical Reflection: "Noel Festival"

Scan the QR Code below to hear the Musical Reflection

11
SILLY SAND

For God so loved the world, that he gave his only begotten Son, that whosoever believeth in him should not perish, but have everlasting life. (John 3:16)

WHEN I THINK of toys at Christmas, one that regularly comes to mind is the gift I never received. When I was a little boy in the early 70's, like most children my age, I made a list and gave it to my parents and to Santa, specifying exactly what presents I wanted that year.

Christmas day 1968 I woke up and ran to the living room and there under the tree was a Tom and Jerry Ukulele, a Bugs Bunny Jack-in-the-Box, and a Mr. Magoo baseball player. 1969: Major Matt Mason, Mattel's Man in Space, and a Frosty the Snowman snow cone maker. 1970: A new bike and the game Operation. As happy as I was to receive those presents, each year I looked for one more. It was a small toy. In fact, I doubt that it even cost one dollar.

It was such a small thing that I never mentioned to my parents. Nor, did I ever write it in a Christmas letter to Santa to make sure he included it under the tree.

It was a simple little craft toy called Silly Sand. You could take different colored sand and squeeze it from a tube into different shapes and creations. I can still remember the tag line of the commercial advertising it each Christmas.

Silly sand is wild, silly sand is wacky, silly sand is wonderful...best of all silly sand is silly....Go ahead get silly...you just can't beat the fun of Silly Sand.

In retrospect I know it doesn't sound that exciting. But that's not the point. Each year I hoped and hoped that Silly Sand would be under the tree. Each year I looked and waited and longed for Silly Sand. But it never came!

And after I had been so good! Each and every year; so respectful to my parents and kind to my brother, so helpful and caring to everyone. And this was the thanks I got, yet one more year without Silly Sand under the tree!

Rather silly, (pardon the pun), don't you think? To place so much emphasis on a little toy; to want and wish for something as trivial as some colored sand. And then to believe for even a moment that the only reason we should receive a special gift is because we have earned it!

But how different is that from the piece of jewelry

or the newest iPhone on our list this year? What gift do you really desire? What gift is it that that you seek this Christmas? Silly Sand? Or a suffering Savior? Let me assure you that the greatest gift of God can't be earned or bought.

A small boy was writing a letter to God about the Christmas presents he badly wanted. "I've been good for six months now," he wrote. But after a moment's reflection he crossed out "six months" and wrote "three". After a pause that was crossed out and he put "two weeks". There was another pause and that was crossed out too. He got up from the table and went over to the little nativity scene that had the figures of Mary and Joseph. He picked up the figure of Mary and went back to his writing and started again: "Dear God, if ever you want to see your mother again...!"

We CANNOT bargain with God to receive the greatest of all gifts. Instead we must simply and humbly come to the Lord and understand the urgency in receiving the gift he has to offer.

You can receive this gift. That's why Jesus came. He didn't come so that we would have an extra holiday. He didn't come so that retail stores could make lots of money during this time of year. He came to be crucified, that through Him, we could go to heaven. He came so that one day, we would not have to stand before God and be sorry. That was his gift at Christmas. Have you received it yet? If you haven't there is no better time than Christmastime.

Prayer: Knowing God, thank you for sending us the gifts we truly need rather than the gifts we think we want. Teach us again that the greatest gifts, Your Greatest Gift, is not something that can be earned but is graciously given. Amen.

Musical Reflection: "God Rest Ye, Merry Gentlemen"

Scan the QR Code below to hear the Musical Reflection

12
SHARING AT CHRISTMAS

(By Mark Hecht Reprinted from Family, Friends, and Faith)

The wilderness and the solitary place shall be glad for them; and the desert shall rejoice, and blossom as the rose. It shall blossom abundantly, and rejoice even with joy and singing: the glory of Lebanon shall be given unto it, the excellency of Carmel and Sharon, they shall see the glory of the Lord, and the excellency of our God. Strengthen ye the weak hands, and confirm the feeble knees. Say to them that are of a fearful heart, Be strong, fear not: behold, your God will come with vengeance, even God with a recompence; he will come and save you. Then the eyes of the blind shall be opened, and the ears of the deaf shall be unstopped. Then shall the lame man leap as an hart, and the tongue of the dumb sing: for in the wilderness shall waters break out, and streams in the desert. And the parched ground shall become a pool, and the thirsty land springs of water: in the habitation of dragons, where each lay, shall be grass with reeds and rushes. And an highway shall be there, and a way, and it shall be called The way of holiness; the unclean shall not pass over it; but it shall be for those: the wayfaring men, though fools, shall not err therein. No lion shall be there, nor any ravenous beast shall go up thereon, it shall not be found there; but the redeemed shall walk there: And the ransomed of the Lord shall return, and come to Zion with songs and everlasting joy upon their heads: they shall obtain joy and gladness, and sorrow and sighing shall flee away. (Isaiah 35:1-10)

The year was 1969 and two young boys knelt and looked through the basement windows of the old church. It was cold outside that early winter evening. Although it was only 5 o'clock, the wintertime sun had already set. The light of the sanctuary shining out through the large stained-glass windows was all that illuminated the night and the two little boys crouched down, silhouetted against the old brick building. A new layer of December snow had fallen and covered the ground with a blanket of white. It was still snowing as the two young boys peered inside that early winter's night.

From where they knelt they could spy a flurry of activity taking place in the basement of that old church building. Dozens of women were moving quickly back and forth through the church kitchen. The boys were used to seeing a lot of activity in that room but this was different. There was no meal being served this evening. And yet there was food everywhere. Bags and bags of canned goods were carried into the room and unpacked on the far counter of the old church kitchen. Along another wall were boxes and boxes filled with oranges and apples. And one by one each piece of fruit was inspected and placed back in the box until one of the women would come and collect a dozen or so of each fruit, bag and carry them to the center of the room to still another box. Next to the boxes of fruit sat tray after tray of Christmas cookies; sugar cookies cut into shapes of wreathes and snowmen, bells and Christmas trees. The boys watched in amazement as several more women carefully packed those cookies into small white boxes, tied them with ribbon and carried them also to the center of the large busy room. Every so often one of the men of the church would enter that kitchen carrying a turkey, and he too would make his way to the center of that room, hand the turkey to another and leave. The activity in that kitchen was energized. Everyone was quickly going about his or her job. They were laughing. You could hear some of them singing Christmas carols. In fact the boys' mother and father were among the busy workers, scurrying about the old church basement.

At the center of that large room, stood several women who were acting differently from the rest. While everyone else was quickly darting back and forth and side to side hand delivering canned goods and turkeys, fresh fruit and cookies, these three ladies at the center of that room, stood calmly behind large empty boxes and gently placed all the other items one at a time into their boxes. Canned goods went in first, a turkey next, fruit on either side, a white box filled with Christmas cookies and tied with a bow carefully positioned on top of the box and then hard Christmas candies and candy canes were sprinkled over the entire contents of the package. Then very carefully large sheets of red or gold cellophane were pulled over the sides of the boxes and tied together at the top with long flowing ribbon.

The two boys were awe struck by the entire spectacle. Never had they seen so much food. And never had they witnessed such care being placed into wrapping and preparing such beautiful packages. When it was finished each box looked like a treasure chest to the young boys. As they watched the adults go about their work that night, they talked with each other about where these wonderful packages must be going. It was obvious that they were very special, so the boys reasoned that they must be presents for very important people. After all it wasn't just anyone who deserved to receive such a beautiful present. Whoever it was that was going to receive those boxes, the one thing the boys did agree upon was that they must be very lucky.

It was not long until the boys' father and mother finished their work and came outside to see the boys and make their way home to their house some six blocks away. The boys quickly told their parents what they had witnessed and how they wished that one day they too might receive a beautiful gift like the ones their parents were helping to prepare.

It was at that moment that their father explained to them that the people who were going to receive those large boxes of food were not the wealthy and powerful but rather the families in need in their church and small town. It was then that the boys' father, *my* father, said to his sons, **"The real joy of Christmas comes in sharing one's best with those who need it most!"** We all went home that night thankful for the experience.

Memories of Christmas. Aren't they wonderful? Thinking about years past, the way things were. What was, as well as what is today, and even what might have been. Christmas is very much about memories, and about being home for the holiday.

We know that more people call home on Mother's Day than any other day of the year. Likewise it is a fact that more people travel home for Thanksgiving than any other holiday of the year. But I would contend that it is Christmas that brings us home like no other holiday ever can. For it is at Christmas time that we remember who we are, and where we come from. We remember the gifts our grandparents made us when we were little. We remember the trips we took to see Santa Claus at the local department store with mom and dad. We remember friends from our childhood and how we once played together building snowmen and snow forts in our yards until it was so cold that we couldn't stand it any longer. We remember sled riding, and caroling, letters to Santa and visits to elderly relatives. And many of us spend time during this holiday remembering friends and loved ones who are no longer with us, except in our hearts.

Yes, it is true more calls are made and more travel done at other times of the year, but it is Christmas that really brings us home again. Not in a physical sense but a spiritual one. For it is Christmas that helps us remember who we are and Whose we are.

I don't know about you, but I believe I am more in touch with my roots at Christmastime than any other. There are more family memories associated with this season, than any other time of year. We use the decorations our parents used when we were younger and remember how they looked in our homes growing up. We spend time using the same recipes our mothers did to make the holiday cookies, so we can even taste our past. And though we may not have realized it at the time, those who went before us, shared what they had and who they were with us because they loved us. And if we were to be honest, we do not always remember things exactly the way they really happened. Time has a way of smoothing over the difficulties, and disagreements, and allowing us to think only of the joy and love that was there.

For **the real joy of Christmas does come in sharing one's best with those who need it most!** Our God knew that. For this is in fact what God did that first Christmas when he sent the baby Jesus into the world. The world did not even recognize it at the time, and yet our collective memories of the story that has been passed down for two thousand years of a baby in a manger come to save us from our sins, help us to be brought home again as well.

Only the home that I speak of now is not the home of our youth or the homes we live in today. Rather the home we are called to is a home with our Lord.

In the scripture lesson from Isaiah, there are words that paint a beautiful picture of the final kingdom in which God will establish justice and destroy all evil. These words speak of a time when glory of the Lord will be seen by all. When the weak will be made strong, the blind will see, the deaf will hear, water will spring forth in the desert, no longer will the ferocious beasts be found… but the redeemed will return to the Lord…they will enter Zion with singing… gladness and joy will overtake them and sorrow and sighing will flee away.

Now when Isaiah speaks these words he is speaking to a people who have endured hardship at the hands of their enemies, and who will continue to do so. He is speaking to a people who have never known the complete peace and joy to which he refers. His is not so much a memory as it is a wish or goal for people of faith. A wish for what might be for the people of faith.... to come home to Zion and worship the Lord.

The person of Jesus Christ makes such peace possible. **The real joy of Christmas comes in sharing one's best with those who need it most!** When we remember the Christ child, we remember a God of Love, who is willing to give us far more than we deserve. For we are still a people who need the forgiveness and salvation that Jesus Christ alone offers.

We are truly blessed, and Christmas helps us recognize that fact like no other time. I came to this realization very early in my own life, in fact it was the Christmas of 1970. A year when my father was laid off work for several months before the holiday and still no full-time job prospects for the future. It was that Christmas that I remember going to the front door of our house and seeing a large cellophane wrapped box of food from a church family that was sharing it's best with those who needed it most!

And when I remember that Christmas I am brought home for the holidays. For when I remember that gift, I remember too, the reason it was given was because a far greater gift was shared with us all in Jesus Christ.

What are your memories? What have you received that brings you home? And more importantly, what might you share with another, to help them know that their God remembers them and desires for them to come home to him.

The real joy of Christmas comes in sharing one's best with those who need it most!

Share your joy. Share your Savior. And welcome home.

> **Prayer:** Giving and Gracious God, You sent Your best that very first Christmas to all of us who need it most. Show us the opportunities to share what you have so generously given to us with those around us in need. Amen.
>
> **Musical Reflection:** "Largo with Hark, the Herald Angels Sing"

Scan the QR Code below to hear the Musical Reflection

13

WINDOW ON MAIN STREET

And suddenly there was with the angel a multitude of the heavenly host praising God, and saying, Glory to God in the highest, and on earth peace, good will toward men. And it came to pass, as the angels were gone away from them into heaven, the shepherds said one to another, Let us now go even unto Bethlehem, and see this thing which is come to pass, which the Lord hath made known unto us.

And they came with haste, and found Mary, and Joseph, and the babe lying in a manger. And when they had seen it, they made known abroad the saying which was told them concerning this child. And all they that heard it wondered at those things which were told them by the shepherds. But Mary kept all these things, and pondered them in her heart. And the shepherds returned, glorifying and praising God for all the things that they had heard and seen, as it was told unto them. (Luke 2:13-20)

APPROXIMATELY A DECADE ago I was doing some early Christmas shopping in late November when I came across and purchased a DVD collection of Christmas episodes from old television shows. Included in the set were *McHale's Navy, The Flying Nun and Father Knows Best*. I purchased the set in the first place to watch the *Father Knows Best* episode starring Robert Young. Robert Young played the father Jim Anderson on the mid-1950's show. After playing that role he would go on to star in yet another popular show in the 1970's as *Marcus Welby MD*. The shows on the DVD did not disappoint, they were sentimental and funny; just what I was looking for.

But included with this little collection was an episode of an obscure show Young made in 1961 that ran on network television for only half of one season. I had never heard of it. Almost everyone I have asked has no recollection of it either. The show was called *Window on Main Street*. Let me encourage you if you ever have the chance, take thirty minutes and enjoy this incredibly beautiful and touching Christmas story.

Robert Young played Cameron Garrett Brooks. Brooks is a middle-aged widower writer who returns to his home town and tells stories about the people in his life. The show was part comedy and part drama. The Christmas episode shares the story of his first Christmas with his wife, who had died tragically a decade or so prior.

His wife Selma, gives him a large wrapped gift for Christmas. Cameron is excited because he thinks it is golf clubs, only to be a bit disappointed when he unwraps it and finds an antique butter churn instead. He and his wife have a good laugh and then she says these words to him from off camera.

"Anything that reminds me of you is beautiful to me. If only we could always be this happy and spend all future Christmases together."

Cameron replies, "What do you mean, if?"

Selma continues, "We never know what is ahead of us really. I have strange feelings about such things. But let's vow that even if for some reason we're apart we'll always spend our Christmases together in spirit. Wherever we are on Christmas Eve, we'll each go out for a walk in the snow and look up at the moon. And there we'll see each other!"

What that little story said to me is that there are all kind of things around us that allow us to celebrate love and opportunities to share it. Christmas time is an opportunity to gather with those who are dear to us. And even if we cannot be together, we can look out into the winter night sky and be thankful for their love.

Prayer: Infinite God, we thank you that you place moments of grace into our lives that later bring back thoughts of people and places that are dear to us. May this be a season where we reflect and remember that those we love are always with us. Amen.

Musical Reflection: "Gesu Bambino"

Link to episode: Window on Main Street
https://youtu.be/woPJExKBHm8

Scan the QR Code below to hear the Musical Reflection

14
THE GIFT OF LOVE

We love him, because he first loved us. (1 John 4:19)

GIFTS AND CHRISTMAS. The two go hand in hand. From a fictitious drummer boy who plays his drum for the baby Jesus because he has no other gift to offer him, to the young child who drops her entire allowance in the Salvation Army kettle in front of the local store to help others in need.

Christmas at its best is about having the proper attitude towards the giving and receiving of gifts. Consider that first Christmas. Shepherds gave up their very livelihoods when they left their sheep, dropped everything and went to search for the baby Jesus. Magi from afar had given their lives to the study of the stars awaiting a sign that the Messiah, the Savior had arrived. And their years of giving were rewarded as they found and followed that star to Jesus.

Once more this season there will appear wonderful presents, wrapped in beautiful paper, tied in ribbons and bows, beneath our Christmas trees. There will be games, and clothes, books, and music, all selected with love and care. But Christmas is the celebration of Jesus' birth. It is a remembrance of what God gave to us. What gift could we give to God that could express our love for Him in return? What do we have under the tree for Jesus?

At our house the gifts we tend to open first are those in the biggest boxes or those with the shiniest paper. The more attractive the packaging the more important we perceive the gift to be. Often times the poorly wrapped boxes, or those without shiny paper or pretty bows sit under the tree for some time before being opened.

I remember the little boy who handed me a balled-up piece of tissue paper after the Christmas Eve worship service thirty years ago. I assumed it was a piece of trash he had picked up and was handing it to me because I was the first adult he saw and wanted to be rid of it. I put it in my pocket as I continued to greet the worshipers leaving church that night. The little boy disappeared quickly and I didn't give him another thought until I was back in my office and putting my robe away I pulled out the balled up paper and out fell a beautiful pipe cleaner angel that had obviously taken much time for his little hands to construct. Tied to the ornament was a note, "To Rev. Hecht. Love, Michael". A heartfelt gift, created with loving hands and given with care was almost cast aside because I was too quick to think it worthless.

Now remember that first Christmas. *Luke 2:7 "and she gave birth to her firstborn, a son. She wrapped him in cloths and placed him in a manger, because there was no room for them in the inn."* The savior of the world was given with care as a heartfelt gift, and was nearly ignored completely.

Let us remember to never judge the gift based upon our own ideas of what it should look like and be. Let us instead judge the value of the gift by the heart of the one who gives it.

There is an ancient story of a medieval monk that was renowned for his preaching skills. Word began to spread that the monk was coming to town to deliver a powerful message on the Love of God. As the day of his coming approached, the town was filled with excitement to hear this amazingly eloquent speaker. On Sunday evening the church was packed, there was great anticipation for what was to come.

As the shadows of night began to fall the monk stepped to the pulpit to deliver his sermon. Before he began however he turned to gaze at the crucifix on the wall behind the pulpit. He paused for a long time. Then he stepped to the altar and took a candle and lit it. He held the candle first to illuminate the crown of thorns on the head of the image of Jesus on the cross. Then he held the candle to the nail scarred hands, and then the feet. Lastly, he held the candle to illuminate the spear pierced side of the savior. As he walked back to the pulpit a holy hush fell on the gathered crowd.

The monk then set the candle on the pulpit, blew it out and quietly left the church. Having never said a word. Ultimately there were no words that could compare to the eloquent expression of love that God expressed through the giving of His Son on the cross.

The question remains, what gift will we bring to Jesus this year? There is a poem I believe helps us in answering that question. It is entitled; **<u>His Name Is At the Top.</u>**

> I had the nicest Christmas list,
> The longest one in town,
> Till Daddy looked at it and said,
> "You'll have to cut it down."
>
> I knew that what he said was true
> Beyond the faintest doubt,
> But was amazed to hear him say,
> "You've left your best Friend out."
>
> And so I scanned my list again,
> And said, "Oh, that's not true!"
> But Daddy said, "His name's not there,
> That Friend who died for you."

And then I clearly understood,
'Twas Jesus that he meant;
For Him who should come first of all;
I hadn't planned a cent!

I'd made a Christmas birthday list,
And left the Savior out!
But, oh, it didn't take me long
To change the list about.

And tho' I've had to drop some names
Of folks I like a lot
My Lord must have the most,
because HIS NAME IS AT THE TOP!

The greatest gift of all was given when Jesus gave his life for us. This Christmas the greatest gift we can give back to God is our life. Trust Him with all of your being and follow him in all that you do. We recognize the wrappings that surround us are often not so beautiful. We know our lives are often times scarred by sin and sadness and we know that sometimes we don't give nearly as much thought to our God as He gives his care to us. Yet none of that need matter. This season we can begin anew. Celebrate the gift given and seek opportunities to love Christ in return.

> **Prayer:** Caring God, Your gifts to us come wrapped in many ways. Enable us to look

beneath the outward appearance to the truth of Your love for us. Amen.

Musical Reflection: "The Gift of Love"

Scan the QR Code below to hear the Musical Reflection

15
THE CHRISTMAS WREATH

> The thief comes only to steal and kill and destroy. I came that they may have life and have it abundantly. (John 10:10)

WHEN I WAS young, Christmas decorating in my family was a well-organized and carefully ordered tradition. Each year, the day after Thanksgiving our family assembled in the living room as my father retrieved from the recesses of the attic and the back corner of the cellar boxes filled with Christmas magic! Large multi-colored lights were attached to the roof line of the house. Dad climbed the ladder as we carefully tightened each bulb and then handed the string to him to fasten to the house. While we were at work outside, Mom was dusting the windowsills and carefully balancing candelabras of electric lights in each of the first-floor windows. My brother and I would fight over who got to hang the Styrofoam Santa head inside the kitchen storm door. Finally, we would all gather on the front porch where together we would twist garland around the wrought iron railings and add more lights to frame the front door. Each year, the order was almost always the same. But it is the memory of the last decoration we would hang that has remained with me all my life.

The final decoration was always the Christmas Wreath! The symbol of the Christmas wreath is important to remember. The shape symbolizes the **crown of thorns** that was placed on the head of Jesus Christ, and the resurrection which offers life eternal to all who believe. The term wreath is derived from the Middle English word, 'wrethe' which means a band. The leaves and fruits in the band symbolize the strength of life.

But why was the wreath the most important decoration on our family home? To answer that question, we need to go back to the year 1945. It was a joyous time for the nation as World War II had ended. For my family, however, it was a year filled with great pain and sorrow. My mother's father had died suddenly on June 30th of that year and as the Christmas holiday approached, her grandfather (the person she was closest to in the entire world) was very ill. Everyone was so concerned with Grandpa's weakening condition that no one thought to decorate even though decorations had been purchased and sat still packed in a box on the front porch. Days of sitting at his bedside turned into weeks filled with prayer as they awaited the inevitable. My Great Grandfather was a man of deep faith. During one of the last conversations my mother remembered having with him, he told her, "Annie, don't be sad because I know that I am going home to be with my Lord." On December 23, 1945 he passed away in his sleep. They were sad but they also knew that he was safe in the Lord's arms.

It was still the custom in that community to have visitation at the house and it was also the tradition to place a black wreath of mourning on the front door. Almost immediately the black wreath appeared, a reminder to the community that death had visited this house. The following day was Christmas Eve. A steady stream of long-faced and saddened neighbors appeared at the house expressing their condolences. The hours passed and it was nearing midnight. My mother and her sister and mother stepped out to the front porch of the house. Snow was falling, church bells were ringing and Christmas was coming. They missed Grandpa but they also remembered his words. "Don't be sad because I know that I am going home to be with my Lord." At that moment one of them reached down and opened the box of decorations on the front porch and pulled out a Christmas wreath; a symbol of life and life eternal. They removed the black wreath from the door and joyfully hung the Christmas wreath in its place.

Jesus came at Christmas that we might have eternal life. Thank God for the gift of His son who turns sorrow into joy and death to life!

> **Prayer:** Life-giving God, you turn our mourning into dancing. We give you thanks that even in those moments when we are at our lowest, we can catch the ray of light that promises the joy that awaits us through Jesus. Amen.
>
> **Musical Reflection:** "Bring a Torch, Jeannette Isabella"

Scan the QR Code below to hear the Musical Reflection

16
MAKING CHRISTMAS JUST RIGHT

And the angel said unto them, fear not: for, behold, I bring you good tidings of great joy, which shall be to all people. For unto you is born this day in the city of David a Savior, which is Christ the Lord. (Luke 2:10-11)

WHAT A CHRISTMAS season it was. Worship services were planned, sermons written, parties scheduled and shopping lists prepared. Everything was going smoothly that year. Yes, I was busy at church and we were busy at home, but everything was running like a well-oiled machine. And then it happened. Out of nowhere...LARYNGITIS! This was not just a minor sore throat. This was not being able to make a sound above a whisper for the better part of three weeks right in the middle of December. What were we going to do? I was frustrated and angry and every other emotion you can imagine. Every one of the church staff and congregation offered their own home remedies and I tried them all. I went to the doctor and took all the prescribed medicines. But being a child of the 1970's I knew what I really needed...I needed a Carol Brady Christmas Miracle.

Remember the Brady Bunch episode in which Carol lost her voice and was to sing the solo on Christmas morning? All it took was little daughter Cindy asking Santa to give her mommy her voice back in time for the big service. Carol awakened Christmas morning and her voice miraculously had returned.

So each morning for two weeks leading up to Christmas Eve I assumed one day, my voice would simply return and all would be well. But the days began to pass and nothing much was happening.

By Christmas Eve I had taken 10 days of antibiotics, 5 days of steroids, 740 cups of tea and approximately two gallons of honey. All so that I could deliver a Christmas Eve sermon with the volume level of just above a whisper. While it was frustrating to me to have no voice at all, my wife Karen is always quick to add that she enjoyed it immensely!

As frustrating as losing my voice was, there were a myriad of other things that failed to go as planned. I am proud to say that I didn't blow a gasket the day I was in line at Walmart in the ten item or less line, mind you, feeling miserable, unable to speak, just wanting to get out and get home. It was in that moment that I found myself behind a woman with 47 items. Yes, she had 47 items. I counted them! Of course, I couldn't say anything even if I wanted to. In some ways it was therapeutic; like counting to a hundred before you say something you shouldn't. In any event, God kept me quiet in that moment even if internally I wanted to scream.

Nor did I lose my cool a few days later, as my voice was slowly returning when I realized I needed to get to the grocery store to buy two packages of butter so I could get some baking done that I had put off because I was feeling so poorly.

I drove to the store, got the butter, stood in line for what seemed like an eternity. I started counting to 47 to myself to attempt to calm down. I finally got to the resister to pay for the butter and go to the end of aisle only to find that the bagger had given my butter to the person in front of me and they had taken it and were walking away. I didn't have enough voice to yell and get their attention so off they went. But that too, was OK. I didn't get upset I just went and got more butter, kept it in my hands this time and made my way home.

Oh, the challenges and frustrations of Christmas when we so desperately want things to go "just right" and it doesn't turn out the way we had intended. It happens to everyone.

Parents drag screaming children out of the toy store. Testy drivers on the road block cars from merging because they want to get to the next store before anyone else. It even happens in church. We rush and growl at the wife and kids to hurry up and get ready for church. We yell at everyone to behave as we speed to service and we arrive so anxious that it is difficult if not impossible to worship. And the crazy thing is that we do these things with the best of intentions. We want things to be perfect. We want Christmas to be "just right" and sometimes in the process, we try so hard to get it just right that someone or everyone ends up in tears and Christmas isn't really Christmas.

If you can relate to any of this, let me now ask you to consider what do you suppose that first Christmas was like? Was everything "just right" for Joseph, Mary and the Baby Jesus? Of course not. Did she really enjoy traveling all the way from Galilee to Bethlehem while nine months pregnant? When it came time for the baby to be born did Mary really want to be giving birth in a cattle shed? No and no again. Isn't it likely at least at some point Mary just broke down and cried because she couldn't make it "just right"?

And maybe that is, in fact, what we are supposed to remember about Christmas. We have Christmas, because WE CAN'T MAKE IT RIGHT! Christmas is the reminder that God comes in the form of a little baby because He wants to and only He can make things right. God takes on human form and comes into our world to restore the brokenness around us and within us. In the baby in the manger God makes things "Just Right."

The angel of the lord proclaimed it. *"Fear not: for, behold, I bring you good tidings of great joy, which shall be to all people." For unto you is born this day in the city of David a Savior, which is Christ the Lord."*

When you get right down to it, Christmas is what makes things right. God sent his son and now he desires to see what we will do. Will we receive him or reject him?

Do you want Christmas to be just right this year? Maybe instead of trying so hard to make the season perfect we simply welcome into our lives, our homes, and our relationships the One who has come to save us. In doing so we can be assured that God will indeed make Christmas "just right"!

> **Prayer:** Justifying God, when all of our plans seem to disintegrate before our eyes, You are able to rearrange the pieces to create an even better plan. Help us to yield to You in those moments and remember how very constant is Your love for us. Amen.
>
> **Musical Reflection:** "Joseph Dearest, Joseph Mine"

Scan the QR Code below to hear the Musical Reflection

17
GRANDMA'S ORNAMENT

Though I speak with the tongues of men and of angels, but have not love, I have become sounding brass or a clanging cymbal, And though I have the gift of prophecy, and understand all mysteries and all knowledge, and though I have all faith, so that I could remove mountains, but have not love, I am nothing. And though I bestow all my goods to feed the poor, and though I give my body to be burned, but have not love, it profits me nothing.

Love suffers long and is kind; love does not envy; love does not parade itself, is not puffed up; does not behave rudely, does not seek its own, is not provoke thinks no evil; does not rejoice in iniquity, but rejoices in the truth; bears all things, believes all things, hopes all things, endures all things.

Love never fails. But whether there are prophecies, they will fail; whether there are tongues, they will cease; whether there is knowledge, it will vanish away. For we know in part and we prophesy in part. But when that which is perfect has come, then that which is in part will be done away.

When I was a child, I spoke as a child, I understood as a child, I thought as a child; but when I became a man, I put away childish things. For now we see in a mirror, dimly, but then face to face. Now I know in part, but then I shall know just as I also am known.

And now abide faith, hope, love, these three; but the greatest of these is love. (1 Corinthians 13)

MY GRANDMOTHER WAS a sweet gentle woman who lived a hard life. And through it all, she continually demonstrated love and care for her family and friends and a deep and abiding faith that gave her great peace in difficult times. Born in June of 1903, she was quite ill and was not expected to live through her first Christmas. Needless to say, she surprised everyone and grew in strength all that year. That Christmas her parents did not have much but still they purchased a single ornament for her. It was a small Victorian baby carriage made of metal and glass, with a baby inside made from pipe cleaners and crepe paper. Every year this ornament was brought out and placed on her tree. As she grew older and had her own family she took the ornament with her and year after year it was one of the many that would be placed on the tree at Christmas. In later years when no longer able to stay by herself because of her declining health she came to live with my parents and my brother and me. The ornament came and decorated our tree; an ornament she ultimately gave to me. As I unpack it, I remember her quiet grace, her love of family, her strong faith in good times and in bad. And I think of the love she passed down from one generation to the next.

As time has passed, it has taken a toll on that ornament. The metal wires began to bend, the glass ball that made up the body of the carriage cracked long ago. One year the remaining part of the pipe cleaner doll that rode atop it, was lost. It has now been more than three decades of Christmas celebrations without my grandmother, yet her ornament still graces our home and this year will help to decorate our family tree for the 120th year! Each and every year as the ornament goes on the tree I remember my Grandmother's love.

I suspect there will come a time when we go to unpack the ornament and it will be reduced to pile of dust. If and when that occurs, I would like to believe I will be alright with that as well. Because the love that was in that gift more than a century ago has been shared with and a part of my life for so long, that no one can take that away from me. In fact, there is joy in passing that love on to others.

It is that kind of love that my grandmother shared with her family that I now continue to share with mine. I attempt to share love with family that has been passed down through generations and still influences them this very day.

We need to remember as we rapidly approach the culminating event of our celebration of the birth of Jesus Christ, to also prepare ourselves for the journey that the savior is going to make to Calvary's cross.

You see, if in fact the ornaments we place on our trees this time of year are symbols of love, then our trees should be covered from top to bottom with crosses! What better symbol of love do we have this time of year or any time of year than the cross.

> For God so loved the world that he gave his only begotten son that whosoever believes in him should not die but have ever lasting life. (John 3:16)

Our faith, like symbols such as the star, the Christmas tree and the cross, often times seem to take a beating anymore. And while it may appear that they are cracking apart and losing their significance to the world, I think about Grandma's old broken ornament. And how it was partially because I hadn't taken care of it that it began to break. Then I remember that it doesn't matter what others might say or do. Even if they fail to recognize it for what it is, I KNOW! And I take that with me wherever I go.

We rally around the flag, we even rally around the Christmas tree, but do we really rally around our faith? Christmas, just like everything else in this world, is what we choose to make of it. Can you take the ornaments/symbols of faith this Christmas season, dust them off no matter how banged or dented they may appear at first and share them with the world?

Christmas is not a secular holiday no matter how much the world might go out of its way to make it just that. Christmas is a time to remember, a time to celebrate, and a time to allow the love of God in the person of Jesus Christ to come into our lives. Religious tolerance is not measured by the lengths to which we are willing to go to make ourselves a nameless, faceless and useless society.

C.S. Lewis once put it this way- "I believe in Christ as I believe in the sun. For I not only see it, but by it I see everything else." What better time of year than now to take the gift that has been passed down to us; the gift of a savior, the gift of faith, the gift of love and look for opportunities to share it with others.

Prayer: Faithful God, the love shown to us through others ornament our lives in special ways. We remember kind words, thoughtful gestures, and acts of generosity. Help us to remember that all of these are reflections of Your great gift in Jesus and His gracious sacrifice on our behalf. Make us truly grateful. Amen.

Musical Reflection: "Coventry Carol"

Scan the QR Code below to hear the Musical Reflection

18
ENTERING THE PICTURE

And she will bring forth a Son, and you shall call His name JESUS, for He will save His people from their sins. (Matthew 1:21)

I REALIZE FOR many it may be difficult to remember a time when we weren't all carrying a smart phone in our pocket to record each and every important and less than important life event that takes place. Some of us remember a day when important events were recorded with Kodak cameras. My father considered himself rather technologically savvy and was quite proud of himself when he purchased his first Polaroid camera. Do you remember those "easy to use" Polaroid cameras that allowed you to have your photo "Instantly"? All one needed to do was take the ten-pound camera out of the suitcase sized carrying case, pop out the bellows, set the lens for the proper distance, take the picture, pull out the paper, wait several minutes, peel off the top layer and after, what seemed like an eternity, apply a coating of toxic smelling liquid....and *voila*! An instant picture!

Regardless of the methods used to acquire and preserve them, I have always loved family photos. I enjoy leafing through album after album remembering my past and sharing it with others. Not long ago, however, while inspecting an album filled with decades worth of family Christmas photos I noted something for the very first time.

Even though there were hundreds of photos in the album, my father was never in any of the pictures! Not one. This might seem disappointing to some. Dad has been gone for over thirty years and I have far fewer pictures to remember him by or to share him with my children and grandchildren than other family members. But this isn't how I see those photos at all! For I remember that he was, in fact, present for every photo. See, I know he was there because he was the one taking all the photos! He was there behind the camera watching, directing and waiting for something to happen.

Now consider what took place in Bethlehem some two thousand years ago. For thousands of years, God the Father was present behind the scene, or at the very least, out of the picture, watching, directing and waiting. Then one Holy Night that we celebrate as Christmas, God the Father "entered the picture." A baby boy reaches out his hand to touch us and bring us closer to himself. And as we come closer to his presence his mother Mary tells us his name is Jesus because he will save us, his people, from our sins. No longer was he on the outside waiting and watching. Instead He came into our world and into our lives in the form of a baby and for that we have reason to rejoice.

> **Prayer:** Immortal, Invisible God, You often move in our lives in unseen ways, nudging us towards Your best for us and away from what would harm us. Focus our thoughts on Jesus as we prepare ourselves to receive this great gift from Your heart. Amen.

> **Musical Reflection:** "How Great Our Joy"

Scan the QR Code below to hear the Musical Reflection

19
MISPLACING JESUS

Now his parents went to Jerusalem every year at the feast of the Passover. And when he was twelve years old, they went up to Jerusalem after the custom of the feast. And when they had fulfilled the days, as they returned, the child Jesus tarried behind in Jerusalem; and Joseph and his mother knew not of it. But they, supposing him to have been in the company, went a day's journey; and they sought him among their kinsfolk and acquaintance. And when they found him not, they turned back again to Jerusalem, seeking him.

And it came to pass, that after three days they found him in the temple, sitting in the midst of the doctors, both hearing them, and asking them questions. And all that heard him were astonished at his understanding and answers. And when they saw him, they were amazed: and his mother said unto him, Son, why hast thou thus dealt with us? behold, thy father and I have sought thee sorrowing. And he said unto them, How is it that ye sought me? wist ye not that I must be about my Father's business? And they understood not the saying which he spake unto them. And he went down with them, and came to Nazareth, and was subject unto them: but his mother kept all these sayings in her heart.

And Jesus increased in wisdom and stature, and in favor with God and man. ((Luke 2:41-52)

HAVE YOU EVER misplaced something? You knew you hadn't lost it, you just could not find it. Maybe it was your wallet, a pen or your car keys. You know what I'm talking about. What do you do when that happens? First off you don't know there's a problem until you need what it is you thought you had. It is not until you go to pay your dinner tab that you reach for your wallet and it's not there. When you are ready to take the number down you realize your pen has vanished in thin air. Or as you hurry out the door to go pick up your child at school and you discover you no longer have your keys. Then what do you do? You begin to retrace your steps so you can find what you have misplaced.

Mary and Joseph had been to Jerusalem to celebrate the feast of Passover, their now twelve-year-old son was with them. When the feast was over they began to travel back home. They had traveled a whole day's journey and made camp that evening before they had realized they had misplaced Jesus. Before you write them off as being bad parents and not keeping track of their child, understand they were traveling in a large group. The women and children generally would begin the journey ahead of the men, seeing how they traveled a little slower. By evening time when they would make camp the men had caught up with the women and children. I am sure Mary thought Jesus was with Joseph. And Joseph assumed Jesus was with Mary. So it was not until that evening they discovered Jesus had been misplaced, and even lost at this point.

I still remember an autumn Sunday afternoon some twenty years ago. Church was over and our family was home watching the Pittsburgh Steelers football game. A door slammed and in walked our 10-year-old son with hands on his hips and a disgusted look on his face. "Thanks! You forgot me at church today!" Our neighbors thankfully brought him home. But not only had we forgotten him, we didn't even notice he was missing!

How far would you have traveled before you realized that you had misplaced Jesus? Or should I ask are you sure Jesus is still with you in your travels? Are you sure you have not misplaced him? When was the last time you felt that you really needed him? When was the last time you had to call on him? When did you call to him in a time of need or come to him to give thanks for a blessing?

There are some people that really don't feel like they need Jesus. Maybe you feel like you are smart enough on your own or strong enough on your own. You'll save Jesus for the "big stuff", you say. There are others that have such a fleeting relationship that they think Jesus is with them but really they have misplaced him and have not realized it yet.

While we are still in the midst of the Advent season, New Years is not that far away. In a few short weeks we will be reflecting once again on what resolutions we will make as we enter a new year. Have you ever noticed that New Year's resolutions look strangely familiar? As a matter of fact, don't they most often look exactly like last year's resolutions?

Too often in this season we look at the resolutions we made for our lives that we never got started. Eat right, exercise, save more, spend less, and by mid-January we are right back to our old habits.

Spiritually, too often we get too far away from the source that gives us life, fuels our spirit, and reveals our soul. We wander and forget. And it doesn't take long. But that is why we take the time to remember what is important and to rediscover the lines we drew for ourselves in the past. I read the story about a man who painted lines in the middle of the road in the days when they did it by hand. He was entered in a contest. The first day he painted five miles of line, which was a new world record. The next day he painted only 500 feet. The next day just 27 feet. Someone asked why. The painter replied, "I kept getting farther and farther away from the bucket." We wander too far from the very source that gives us life and fuels our very being. We wander too far from the things that are most important.

And for some of us this happens in a matter of minutes, hours or days. For others it takes place over a lifetime. Needless to say, it doesn't matter if we mark the time with a stopwatch or a calendar, we all find ourselves at some point, adrift and far away from the one who can give our life real meaning.

For people of faith, that is Jesus (Emmanuel) the baby from the manger and the savior from the cross. So the simple question for us to consider is this: "Do you know where Jesus is for you today?"

It took me some time to understand this truth from Mother Teresa: "There are no big deals anymore, just small things to be done with great love."

I don't know what the future will look like for you. Will there be challenges and trials? Hopefully they are few and far between but if they do occur know that God is with you. Will there be moments of joy and celebration? I hope you find more than you presently expect.

But the reality is that most of this coming year will be spent in ordinary time. In fact, according the liturgical calendar we will soon enter into the season on the church calendar marked as "ordinary time." What a good prophetic note: most of the good that will be done will be done in ordinary time, when no one is looking and no one will report it to the paper.

It won't be long until a new year arrives full of ordinary time. In the middle of ordinary time, know that God comes with extraordinary moments that make all others bearable, believable, and worthwhile.

And remember, we cannot do it alone. We need the one who has come into the world to show us love, to show us the way and to show us how to live. We need Christ to go with us into this ordinary time. Even if we don't spend the majority of every waking moment thinking about him, we still need him and the more we forget about him and our relationship to him the more we run the risk of losing it all.

It won't be long until we are putting the decorations away. Remember when you do, to not put Jesus away or more importantly forget him altogether!

> **Prayer:** Ever present God, if we find ourselves feeling as though something is missing during this season of preparation, remind us that it just might be Jesus. Redirect us to Him as the source of our joy. Amen.

> **Musical Reflection:** Thou Didst Leave Thy Throne

Scan the QR Code below to hear the Musical Reflection

20

NATIVITY SCENES

The Lord himself will give you a sign: The virgin will be pregnant. She will have a son, and she will name him Immanuel. (Isaiah 7:14)

I WAS RETURNING from a ten-day mission trip to Haiti. It was an emotionally and physically draining experience, but I felt blessed to have seen God at work in some amazing ways while there. We arrived at the airport and were awaiting our departure. I had a moment to stop in one of the small gift shops at the airport where a small Haitian nativity scene was pointed out to me by one of our group. I really liked it and asked the saleswoman how much it was. She told me…but then she said…she had several more of them…only they didn't have the baby with them. She then assured me that she could give me a really good deal on one of them. I tried ever so tactfully to explain, that the Baby…as she referred to Jesus, was the whole point of the set and without him...it really wasn't worth anything.

Nativity scenes, or crèches, have ancient origins. The popularity of nativity scenes is due however, to St. Francis who reenacted what was the first living nativity. When St. Francis visited Rome in 1223, he asked for permission from Pope Honorius III to hold a special celebration during Christmas. He constructed a nativity and around it stood figures of Mary and Joseph, the donkey, the ox, and the shepherds who came to adore the new-born Savior. On Christmas night a child was placed in a crib as an ox and donkey stood nearby.

The idea of a having a nativity scene, was immediately popular. Initially, churches were the only ones that erected nativity scenes during Christmas, but soon the more affluent and prominent citizens began having their own created. The tradition has continued for hundreds and hundreds of years.

Everywhere you look these days, there are nativity scenes: mangers with Mary and Joseph and the baby Jesus, shepherds and even Wise Men complete with camels. Some of the more elaborate sets include figures that are not in the biblical story, but which come from the legends and plays of the Middle Ages, such as a beggar and a thief and a flute boy, a little drummer boy and even the innkeeper and his wife. The Wise Men show the three ages of man: youth, middle age, and old age and are of different colors: white, darker complexioned, and black, suggesting that this child is for all people. Even an angel or two are present, though the angels, Luke tells us, appeared in the fields and not in the stable.

A nativity scene more so than any other decoration in our homes reminds us that Christmas is truly about the giving and receiving of a very special and precious gift. The gift of the Christ child is a gift for all humanity. He has come to and for one and all.

So Christmas is almost here. Most of us have decorated with all the beautiful Christmas lights and Christmas decorations. Our Christmas trees are trimmed and have presents under them. But unless you have had made room for Jesus Christ for this holiday season, your Christmas will be incomplete.

Some have already purchased the finest Christmas gifts for their loved ones for Christmas Day. Some have been singing and playing all the well-known Christmas songs since the day after Halloween! But still, you cannot have a true Christmas unless you have made room for "The Baby", Jesus Christ.

Some have already gone to numerous parties and have already eaten many Christmas cookies, Christmas cake, and have drunk all the egg-nog they could. But still, you cannot have a true Christmas unless you have made room for Jesus Christ.

Some have plans to travel far and wide during this Christmas season to be with relatives, friends and loved ones. You may even be inviting all of your family, friends, and loved ones over to your house for a Christmas dinner. But still you cannot have true Christmas unless you have Christ.

There is nothing wrong with decorating your house with all the pretty lights and all the decorations for the Christmas holiday season. There is nothing wrong with decorating your Christmas tree so pretty for the Christmas holidays. There is nothing wrong with buying and receiving gifts, or singing the Christmas songs, or going to Christmas parties, eating and drinking the Christmas goodies, inviting people over to your house for Christmas dinner or traveling to see family and friends during the Christmas holidays. No, there is nothing wrong with doing some of these things this Christmas holiday season. But your Christmas would be incomplete if you do not make room for Jesus Christ. WITHOUT THE BABY it's all WORTHLESS!

Did you ever notice how in most nativity scenes all the figures are supposed to do the exact same thing? They are all to be looking towards the baby! What a great reminder.

You see, Jesus Christ should be the focal point of our Christmas celebrations, and if He is then our celebrations should be about showing love, kindness, care, gentleness, and peace to others. Our celebrations should include a desire to be in harmony with one another, sharing with one another, and praising

God for His Son Jesus Christ because He is the reason for the season.

There are some people who will try to argue and debate about the birthdate of Jesus Christ saying that he was not born on December 25th. But the importance is not in knowing if Jesus was born on December 25th or April 1. The importance is in knowing and believing that He was born. You see, over 2000 years ago, Jesus Christ was born in a city called Bethlehem. When He was born, it was not in a hospital like most of us, but He was born in a stable, in a manger, where all the animals slept because the scripture says that there was no room for them (Mary, Joseph, and newborn baby Jesus) in the inn.

And because he entered this world, we are all offered the opportunity to accept him into our lives.

One of the great debates in some households is whether or not the wise men should be in our nativity scene displays during advent or wait until Epiphany and the twelve days of Christmas to come before placing them there. I remember a number of years ago, realizing that most times I had already started to pack up the decorations, including the nativity scene, before the wisemen would even have arrived!

I know families that do not place the baby Jesus into the manger until Christmas Eve. And I do not mean to spoil any traditions your family may have, but let me offer the following. Jesus came into the world in the form of a baby to be with us. Not just for one day but for every day of our life. Therefore, it seems right that He should be present in that scene always. And we would do well to remember that He came not just for one of us but for all people so the wisemen need to be there as well. And He didn't come for just a month in December, He came for all time. And I can tell you that if you come to our home at any point in the year you will find no less than six nativity scenes out year round, to remind us that the little baby Jesus is EMMANUEL...GOD WITH US... ALWAYS.

> **Prayer:** Loving God, while all the figures we place around the manger have a role to play in telling Your story, help us to always keep our eyes and our hearts turned to Jesus, our hope and our salvation. Amen.

Musical Reflection: "Manger Medley"

Scan the QR Code below to hear the Musical Reflection

21
THE LIVING NATIVITY

And she brought forth her firstborn son, and wrapped him in swaddling clothes, and laid him in a manger; because there was no room for them in the inn. (Luke 2:7)

THE OLD CHURCH sat almost exactly in the middle of downtown. It had been witness to much over the course of its long storied history. Situated in a part of town that had changed tremendously over the years, the world seemed very different now. Once an affluent section of the city, across from the finest department store in town, a block away from the Ivy League club where everybody who was anybody met to socialize. This was the church that had served businessmen, people of power and means for the better part of two hundred years. Families, *important* families, would travel from the edge of the city and beyond just to attend worship there every week.

Once upon a time, many years ago, no one seems to remember exactly when, the members of the congregation thought it a good idea to share with the citizens of their fair city the true message of Christmas by staging and performing a live nativity on the walk in front of their prestigious church. Every evening from 7 to 8 for two full weeks prior to Christmas, the steps in front of the church were transformed into a cattle stall in Bethlehem. Elaborate costumes were made for the three magi from the east, beautiful clothes were chosen for Mary to wear, convincing attire was assembled for Joseph and the shepherds as well. The same script was used for decades. Four times each evening a narrator read into a microphone broadcast above the bustle of the city, the fifteen-minute story of the nativity as the actors pantomimed their parts. There was a solemnity and grandeur to their performances. Each person participating took seriously his or her role. Shepherds bowed and Kings knelt and Mary and Joseph prayed before a baby in a manger as buses and trolleys, pedestrians on their way home from work and shoppers on their way to department stores would stop and watch. The scene was so magical and breath taking it couldn't help but draw one's attention. And each Christmas season, if only for a few brief moments, the people of the city were reminded of the true meaning of the holiday.

Many years had passed. The elite of the city no longer called this church their home. The children of members no longer felt the need to come the whole way in from the suburbs each Sunday to worship there; instead opting for newer churches closer to home. Socials for the elite were no longer held in the large church fellowship room. The room sat empty for months on end. The basement of the old church now housed a shelter for homeless women every night of the year. The department store across the street had long ago closed its doors, empty storefronts and boarded windows had taken the place of Christmas displays and twinkling lights. The trolleys were gone and the street was much darker these days. Far fewer people made their way past the old church. They often avoided that street all together, after all "that's where those homeless people hang out isn't it? It really isn't safe you know!"

Dozens of people sat in pews that once held hundreds. The world and city were different now. Nothing was the same. Everything had changed. Everything, except the annual LIVING NATIVITY.

Somehow, even as the economic situation of the city had shifted, and the exodus to the suburbs had continued, even as membership and attendance steadily declined and other areas of church life vanished, the LIVING NATIVITY continued to be performed each and every year. Several things happened, however, over the course of time, dare I say that made the LIVING NATIVITY even more special.

Since there were no longer enough members to perform each evening, invitations were given to youth and others in the surrounding neighborhoods of the city to come to share in the joy of the season. Young African American youth from the Hill District came one night, on another evening the cast was made up of the sons and daughters of laid off factory workers from the city's Southside. On yet another occasion the group of rather sheltered and naïve kids from a well-to-do suburb came on a lark to attempt their hand at performing the living nativity.

The costumes were now quite tattered. There was no money in the church budget for new outfits, so year in and year out the same old robes were used for shepherds, sheets and other pieces of cloth were sewn and tied together for Mary and Joseph . Even the costumes for the kings were worn in spots, and badly in need of repair.

Because each night a new group came to participate they were unfamiliar with the history and importance of the event in which they were now going to participate. It was not uncommon for fights to break out as one young man kidded another over the bathrobe outfit he was wearing. Other youth participated with fear because they were not used to coming to this part of the city and it was all so new and foreign to them. Still others thought the whole thing was a joke and only half listened as directions were given.

The steps of the church and the street in front of it were often populated by dozens of homeless women waiting for the shelter to open in the church basement. Few shoppers passed that way any more. More often than not it was partiers on their way to another bar. And while there was less activity on the street, the noise level and harshness of the city had actually risen.

You wouldn't think in the midst of so much change, confusion and discomfort that the performance of the LIVING NATIVITY was all that important. But nothing could be further from the truth. For without fail, every night as the seven bells of the old church clock rang out, the microphone was turned on, and the Narrator began to read the words, *"And it came to pass in those days. that there went out a decree from Caesar Augustus that all the world should be taxed."* And later on, *"Fear not for I bring you good tidings of great joy. For unto you is born this day in the city of David a Savior which is Christ the Lord!"*

And youth who one moment before had been fighting and yelling or laughing and joking, made their way down a dirty street in old clothes amidst society's outcasts, (a scene probably far closer to the first Christmas than we would like to believe) and knelt before a broken plastic baby in a cardboard manger with all the seriousness and reverence and awe that you can imagine.

The scene was magical and breath taking. Amazingly, it still drew everyone's attention. And each night, if only for a few brief moments, the people of the city were once again reminded of the true meaning of the holiday.

How and why did that happen? For no other reason than this. When we encounter the Christ child, our lives and world are changed. We are transformed. The silliness and frustrations, fear and even anger of the rest of our lives can melt away when we come to Jesus. Look for and find the baby Jesus who has come to save us, your life will be transformed. Thank God for a Nativity that still lives in our hearts and lives.

> **Prayer:** Gentle God, Your entrance into our busy and noisy lives is so quiet that we may at times not even notice. Open our eyes and ears, calm our hearts so that even in the midst of all else that calls for attention we can humbly kneel before the manger and hear the tidings of great joy. Amen.

Musical Reflection: "O Come, All Ye Faithful"

Scan the QR Code below to hear the Musical Reflection

22

ARE WE THERE YET?

Now when Jesus was born in Bethlehem of Judaea in the days of Herod the king, behold, there came wise men from the east to Jerusalem, saying, "Where is he that is born King of the Jews? for we have seen his star in the east, and are come to worship him."

When Herod the king had heard these things, he was troubled, and all Jerusalem with him. And when he had gathered all the chief priests and scribes of the people together, he demanded of them where Christ should be born.

And they said unto him, "In Bethlehem of Judaea: for thus it is written by the prophet, "And thou Bethlehem, in the land of Juda, art not the least among the princes of Juda: for out of thee shall come a Governor, that shall rule my people Israel."

Then Herod, when he had privily called

the wise men, enquired of them diligently what time the star appeared. And he sent them to Bethlehem, and said, "Go and search diligently for the young child; and when ye have found him, bring me word again, that I may come and worship him also."

When they had heard the king, they departed; and, lo, the star, which they saw in the east, went before them, till it came and stood over where the young child was. When they saw the star, they rejoiced with exceeding great joy.

And when they were come into the house, they saw the young child with Mary his mother, and fell down, and worshipped him: and when they had opened their treasures, they presented unto him gifts; gold, and frankincense and myrrh.

And being warned of God in a dream that they should not return to Herod, they departed into their own country another way. (Matthew 2:1-12)

IT'S JUST A few short days until Christmas and we might easily find ourselves asking the question, now that it's almost done with, "What next"? Or, "Where do we go from here"?

Anyone who has ever been part of a family knows the most commonly asked question on any trip.

Whether it is a vacation across country or a quick run to the grocery store, the most commonly asked question by young people especially is "Are we there yet?"

In our family it was not unusual for the question to be raised before we even got to the end of the driveway. My father's standard answer to the question was, "It's just over the next hill." It always took forever, however, to get to that next hill. Let me point out that this is not an inappropriate question to ask. Asking the question is a clear indication that one is looking forward to arriving. When we go on vacation we anticipate reaching our destination because we believe that not until we reach it can we really enjoy ourselves.

When I was twelve years old my family planned a vacation to Disney World in Florida. At the time I thought that Disney World would be the greatest vacation imaginable. Unfortunately, that meant a several days car ride both down and back from Pennsylvania.

We packed the car, picked up our AAA trip-tik and began our journey. I remember being very impatient as we went through and visited sites on the way down the coast. We passed through Washington DC, Richmond, Virginia, Stone Mountain, Georgia with a side trip to Plains, Georgia to see the birthplace of Jimmy Carter and visit his brother Billy Carter's gas station (my father was a lifelong Democrat!), then to

St. Augustine and just when it seemed we would never arrive; we arrived in Orlando and Disney World.

It felt as though we would never get there. But we did. And after several days we packed our things and started home. To this day I remember very little of Disney World but the stops along the way are very clear; Walking through the Smithsonian Institution in Washington, the Wright brother's plane at Kitty Hawk, Stone Mountain, Georgia, the sun rise on the Atlantic Ocean at St. Augustine are as vivid in my memory over forty years later as the day I first experienced them.

Two thousand years ago wisemen, astrologers from the east were on their own kind of journey filled with expectations and excitement. Actually, it was not just a journey but a pilgrimage. There is a very big difference between taking a journey and going on a pilgrimage. A journey is defined as travel from one place to another and a sojourner as one who lives temporarily as on a visit. A pilgrim on the other hand is defined as a person who travels to a holy place as a religious act. We might also add that a pilgrim brings something along with him or her. They bring along a faith or belief in something. Nothing is required of an individual on a journey except to pass from place to place. A pilgrimage requires intent and faith and hope and anticipation and emotion. The wisemen, we are told, come to find the baby Jesus bearing gifts of gold, frankincense, and myrrh.

On a pilgrimage, one cannot travel empty handed or empty hearted. A pilgrim carries with him or her a faith. One pilgrimages to a place because of what they would like to become, and in hopes of strengthening or renewing their beliefs. There is a sense of planning and order that comes with making a pilgrimage. Our wisemen charted the stars and planned for their trip to see this newborn king. There is a reason for doing what they doing.

We are told that these wisemen were in search of the one born "King of the Jews". The Jews themselves had anxiously anticipated the coming of a messiah for centuries. They were a people who had faced oppression and pain for hundreds of years and prayed that a leader would come to set them free. Possibly these men were Gentile converts to Judaism. They hear of the birth of Jesus and wish to see him. Naturally they would assume the king of the Jews would be born in Jerusalem, King David's royal city. So they make their long pilgrimage to Jerusalem in hopes of seeing the king. But when they arrive they are told that the Christ was to be born in Bethlehem to fulfill the words written by the prophet.

> And you o Bethlehem in the land of Judah are by no means least among the rulers of Judah for from you shall come a ruler who will govern my people Israel. (Micah 5:2)

Just imagine the anticipation and excitement that must have been in their hearts as they made their pilgrimage to Jerusalem. We have no indication of how long it took for the wisemen to arrive but it quite possibly could have taken up to two full years! In any case, it must have seemed long but the closer they got the more excited they must have become, only to be told when they arrived that in fact the king of the Jews was not there.

They prepared themselves again and followed the star in the east that went before them. And when it came to rest over the place where Jesus was, they rejoiced with great joy because their journey had ended!

The wisemen had assumed their journey had ended in Jerusalem, when in fact it had only begun!

God made a journey that Christmas day when God came into the world in the form of a baby, a Messiah, that had come to save the world. In this case it was the people, the Jews, who expected anxiously the coming of their king.

But no matter how much the people wished for God's coming, the decision to make the journey, the decision to become human and save humanity from its sins, was ultimately God's own to make. God journeyed into the world in the form of a babe that Christmas day.

Unfortunately, the baby that came, who journeyed into the world would not be the Messiah the people expected or wanted. While the baby Jesus came to love, they wanted a Messiah that would conquer with the sword. And so begins yet another journey.

It would not be enough to bring love into the world through the birth of a babe. No, this journey would take some 33 years to the cross of Calvary. This would be a journey filled with love demonstrated in the works and words of one who loved us so much he was willing to die for us that we might live.

The weeks of Advent go quickly and it will not be long until we find ourselves on the other side of the Christmas holiday. But never forget that the journey does not end on the 25th of December.

Don't be like the wisemen who were really not very wise and think for a moment that the journey is complete. In fact, we have truly just begun. As far off as it may seem to us today, Easter is just over the next hill.

Whether it be vacation trips, or anticipation of Christmas Day, remember that some of the fondest and dearest and most memorable moments of any journey come from the journeys themselves not in the arriving. I can't tell you the number of people I have talked to who say that Christmas Eve is their favorite time of year and that Christmas Day is always somewhat of a letdown. The excitement of the journey is never quite fulfilled in the actuality of the celebration itself. Perhaps if we were to remember that in the journey to Christmas Day we are only beginning a much greater pilgrimage to Easter, our excitement might be heightened rather than crushed.

Remember that on a pilgrimage, the pilgrim does not come empty handed or empty hearted. What will you bring with you through this Advent season? Is it something that you can continue to carry throughout the coming year? Is it a hope of buying all the right gifts, or of surviving the busyness? Is it an adoration of a God who would do whatever needed to be done in order to forgive the world of its sins? Is it a hope for love and healing in a world that is so unwilling to forgive?

Remember, God came into the world and journeyed through this life for us! So now we continue on to the manger to begin a journey to the cross. Are we there yet? No not yet, but through Christ and with Christ we can all continue the pilgrimage and we can all arrive safely.

> **Prayer**: Accompanying God, remind us that we are not following an itinerary, but joining you on a pilgrimage. Allow us to take only what we need but to make the journey with great anticipation of the Gift that only You can give us. Amen.
>
> **Musical Reflection**: "I Saw Three Ships"

Scan the QR Code below to hear the Musical Reflection

23
TAPESTRY
(BY JANET LORD)

I praise you, for I am fearfully and wonderfully made. Wonderful are your works; that I know very well. My frame was not hidden from you, when I was being made in secret, intricately woven in the depths of the earth. Your eyes beheld my unformed substance. In your book were written all the days that were formed for me, when none of them as yet existed. (Psalm 139: 14-16 NSRV)

SINCE RETIREMENT, AND especially during the quarantine days of 2020, I've had a lot of time to indulge in counted cross-stitch, one of my favorite hobbies. It's just the kind of complicated, tedious work that I love and I find it strangely meditative for me. The patterns are often complicated. Every color has a corresponding symbol. Those symbols are mapped out on a grid to be followed when stitching on the canvas. While the overall picture is important, I can only create it by working on one small area at a time. At times I find myself wondering what a certain color is doing in a certain section, and at those times I need to trust that the designer knows best. And finally, it's CROSS-stitch: each and every stitch is a mini-cross. The final project is made up of a variety of colors, each bearing the mark of the cross, blended together into a magnificent tapestry.

The Oxford Unabridged Dictionary defines a tapestry as "A fabric decorated with designs of ornament or pictorial subjects, painted, embroidered, or woven in colors, used for wall hangings, curtains, to hang from windows or balconies, on festive occasions." At one time tapestries were quite common things to find in the home. Heirlooms, if you will, that were passed down from generation to generation, used to decorate the house, or placed out at special times to celebrate the holidays.

In any case, when one pictures a tapestry, one likely pictures something very valuable or at least something of great sentimental value. Our Christmas memories are themselves kinds of tapestries that we can pull out at Christmas time and share with one another.

If we were to look at our own lives as though it were a tapestry, we would find that each and every one of us had a different picture or design woven into the fabric of our lives. We would each have stories about choices we made good and bad, right and wrong, of the people that shaped our lives, of the joys we experienced, and even the pains and losses we felt.

But if we were to look very closely we would find that the thread that is woven into each of our individual lives is very much the same. In fact, there is a common thread that ties them all together. And that is what we celebrate during the Advent season and hopefully each and every day of our lives. That thread is Jesus Christ, and the fact that he lived and died to show us how to love. The thread that ties us all together is love!

Many years ago the choir presented a cantata entitled, "A Christmas Tapestry" by David Clydesdale and Claire Clonninger. There is a line in the cantata that I believe speaks volumes. It is a line that Mary sings to the baby Jesus, and I believe that it is a loud testament to our lives and to our faith. It says "for our lives have been woven together, we are a part of each other". May this Christmas, be a time for you to bring out and celebrate the tapestries of your lives. For indeed our lives have been woven together, we can be a part of each other." Open your hearts this day and always to the love of God and to the love of all.

Prayer: Designing Lord, we are so grateful for all of the intricate ways in which You have knit us together to better serve you.

Remind us that in Your plan for our lives, You alone see the entire picture. Allow us to rest in that assurance. Amen.

Musical Reflection: "Good Christian Men, Rejoice!"

Scan the QR Code below to hear the Musical Reflection

24
LULLABIES AND MORNING PRAISE

And when eight days were accomplished for the circumcising of the child, his name was called JESUS, which was so named of the angel before he was conceived in the womb. And when the days of her purification according to the law of Moses were accomplished, they brought him to Jerusalem, to present him to the Lord; (As it is written in the law of the LORD, Every male that openeth the womb shall be called holy to the Lord;) And to offer a sacrifice according to that which is said in the law of the Lord, A pair of turtledoves, or two young pigeons.

And, behold, there was a man in Jerusalem, whose name was Simeon; and the same man was just and devout, waiting for the consolation of Israel: and the Holy Ghost was upon him. And it was revealed unto him by the Holy Ghost, that he should not see death, before he had seen the Lord's Christ. And he came by the Spirit into the temple: and when the parents brought in the child Jesus, to do for him after the custom of the law,

Then took he him up in his arms, and blessed God, and said,

"Lord, now lettest thou thy servant depart in peace, according to thy word:

For mine eyes have seen thy salvation, Which thou hast prepared before the face of all people;

A light to lighten the Gentiles, and the glory of thy people Israel."

And Joseph and his mother marveled at those things which were spoken of him.

And Simeon blessed them, and said unto Mary his mother, "Behold, this child is set for the fall and rising again of many in Israel; and for a sign which shall be spoken against;

(Yea, a sword shall pierce through thy own soul also,) that the thoughts of many hearts may be revealed."

And there was one Anna, a prophetess, the daughter of Phanuel, of the tribe of Aser: she was of a great age, and had lived with an husband seven years from her virginity; And she was a widow of about fourscore and four years, which departed not from the temple, but served God with fastings and prayers night and day. And she coming in that instant gave thanks likewise unto the Lord, and spake of him to all them that looked for redemption in Jerusalem.

And when they had performed all things according to the law of the Lord, they returned into Galilee, to their own city Nazareth. (Luke 2:21-39)

I ADMIT IT. When it comes to Christmas I am as sentimental a person as there is. Really, I am. I get choked up every time Jimmy Stewart and Donna Reed embrace at the end of *It's A Wonderful Life* as angel Clarence gets his wings. I want to cheer each year as the U.S. post office delivers bags full of letters to the court house in *Miracle on 34th Street* to help prove to little Natalie Wood and all of New York city that there is a Santa Clause. And I smile each time little Linus Van Pelt stands on an empty stage and recites from memory the Christmas story found in the gospel of Luke to remind Charlie Brown and all his friends the true meaning of the holiday.

Christmas, perhaps more so than any other time of year, is a holiday that allows us, perhaps forces us to remember our past. Isn't that what this time of year is really all about? Remembering! Reflecting back upon what has been with fondness and joy in our hearts, even as we participate once more in the hustle and bustle that is Christmas this year. We hang decorations on our trees that hung on the trees of our youth. We use cookie recipes passed down from Grandma, whether we trim the tree three weeks before Christmas or on Christmas Eve, we likely do so because it's the way we have always done it. All these events and so many more allow us the opportunity to celebrate the moment here and now even as they enable us to remember what once was with great fondness.

Of course, we see it time and again in the songs we sing. Every song this time of year, religious or secular, stirs within us a memory. We sing "Silent Night" and remember every Christmas Eve worship service ever attended with family. I hear the children's song "The Friendly Beasts" and I am transported back to Mrs. Wesley's third grade class when I sang the part of the donkey!

The reality is that the songs of Christmas are intended to help us remember. And I believe this has the been the case since that very first Christmas. Nowhere is this more evident than in the songs of praise found in this scripture. For in the joy-filled responses of Simeon and Anna we see and hear the joy of celebrating the moment even as they reflect upon the past.

At first glance this passage may appear quite contradictory. In it we encounter two different believers, both of whom have apparently awaited the coming of a Messiah for many, many years. Additionally, their individual responses to his arrival are seemingly quite different.

Note how Mary, Joseph and the baby encounter Simeon who is described as a righteous and devout man. He instinctively recognizes the baby Jesus for who he really is and takes the child in his arms and praises God.

> "Master now you are dismissing your servant in peace, according to your word; for my eyes have seen your salvation, which you have prepared in the presence of all peoples; a light for revelation to the Gentiles and for glory to your people Israel."

What Simeon is saying is; "God, I remember your promises. I have lived a long life, and you have always been faithful. You have watched over me and loved me, and you have done for me what you said you would. Because of this I can depart because you have shown me what I have been waiting for, the Messiah!"

They next encounter Anna, also great in age. She never left the temple but stayed there night and day worshiping God. When she sees the child, the scriptures tell us she begins to praise God and to speak about him to all who were looking for the redemption of Jerusalem. In other words, this woman who has waited so long for the Messiah finally sees him and then starts preaching and telling others about him!

Initially it appears these two are singing very different songs. One a lullaby and the other a song of morning praise. When we think of lullabies we think of soothing songs of assurance and rest, words which promise that one is being watched over and protected and will continue to be so all through the night.

On the other hand, a song of morning praise, is a celebration, a proclamation, of all that God has done and has provided. Such songs are confident and filled with rejoicing and praise!

For one the coming of the Christ Child is an ending. "I have seen him now I may sleep. And I do so because God is a God who keeps his promises." For the second, his coming is a beginning. "I have seen him! Now I must share him with others as I praise my God!"

What they have in common is that both Simeon and Anna each recognize the child for who he really is as both know that it is necessary to have Christ in one's life in order to be fulfilled. Further, both affirm if you want peace in your life you should desire to fill your being with Christ because Jesus shows us love and shows us God and shows us how to live.

When you get right down to it, there isn't much difference in their songs after all. I would contend we need to hear both. One isn't truly complete without the other. The assurance of God's presence through the night and the praise and thanksgiving that comes in the morning are really two sides of the same coin. Together they celebrate God's presence and promise in the past as they celebrate the moment here and now.

Have you ever considered that many of the songs we sing at Christmas are also lullabies AND songs of praise?

> Silent Night Holy Night, All is calm all is bright.

> Away in a manger no crib for a bed the little lord Jesus lay down his sweet head.

> What child is this who laid to rest on Mary's lap is sleeping?

Each a comforting message of God's love in Christ come into the world. On the other hand:

> Joy to the World the Lord is come, let earth receive her king

> Go tell it on the Mountain, over the hills and everywhere, Go tell it on the Mountain that Jesus Christ is Lord!

> On this day earth shall ring with the song

children sing, to the Lord Christ the King, born on earth to save us, peace and love he gave us.

Here are the confident words of celebration and praise. Together with the lullabies of the season, they enable followers to truly worship Emmanuel, a God who is with us.

Our nephew Teddy was born on Christmas day. I remember when Karen's sister Linda was expecting, and at the time we had two children. She and her husband Marc were worn out from all the preparations for the new arrival; getting the room ready, buying clothes and car seat, high chair and stroller, baby proofing the house, the list went on and on. I remember the day she said to us that she was really looking forward to the time when the baby would arrive so that all the work would done! We didn't have the heart to tell her the truth, which she soon found out for herself. It had only just begun.

Isn't it funny how we can view so many events in this life as either endings or beginnings, as reasons to rest or opportunities to act! The birth of a child, taking a new job that forces us to move to a new town, and perhaps the best example of all, Christmas itself.

Many of us have already heard friends or family exclaim, "Not Christmas already!" Some are already proclaiming "I'll be glad when it's over!" As if their only goal is to survive another Christmas. So often we think that once the 25th comes and goes that Christmas is over. So we hurry up to celebrate the season:

Buy the presents...done.
Make the cookies...done.
Send the cards...done.
Decorate the tree...done.
Wrap the gifts...done.
Stuff the turkey...done.
Attend worship...done.

We rush through the season, welcome the Christ child, and hurriedly pack up the ornaments and trimmings, finish the last of the cookies and get back to our everyday lives.

But when we do that we miss the message of Christmas. We forget the songs of Christmas; the lullabies of assurance and the morning praise of celebration. We forget that Christ came into the world not only for a moment in time, not even for just one day but for all eternity! And when we welcome him into our lives at Christmas we should do so ready to have him there every moment of every day of our lives.

Let us endeavor to be like Simeon, and use this time of year to reflect back and remember the beauty and love God has shown us in the season and in other places in this life. And thank God for God's abiding presence each and every day. But we cannot stop there. We also need to be like Anna. Once we meet the Christ Child we need to become so excited that we desire to tell others about him. The beautiful story made known to us on a silent and holy night must be told over the mountains and everywhere! Anna knew something we would do well to remember. The celebration does not end with Jesus' birth, it only just begins.

This year as you move through the days of Advent and Christmas, and the business and busyness of the season run their course, remember the songs of the Christmas: songs that remind us that our God keeps his promises, is with us, loves us and wants for us to share that love with others. And, never stop singing!

> **Prayer:** Holy God who give us a song to sing, encourage us to burst forth with all of the joy that this season brings so that others can't help but to join in Your unending hymn. Amen.
>
> **Musical Reflection:** "Canon de Noel"

Scan the QR Code below to hear the Musical Reflection

25

WHY WORSHIP MATTERS

> In the beginning was the Word, and the Word was with God, and the Word was God. The same was in the beginning with God. All things were made by him; and without him was not anything made that was made. In him was life; and the life was the light of men. And the light shineth in darkness; and the darkness comprehended it not. (John 1:1-5)

I HAVE CONCLUDED that the first and last truly selfless act took place in a manger in Bethlehem 2000 years ago when God entered the world in the form of a baby. Why is it so difficult to give of ourselves? And is it possible that we might find a way to make "giving" a tradition in our relationships with others?

Obviously, Christmas is a time filled with family traditions. Everything from the decorating of the

Christmas tree to the baking of Christmas cookies has "history" behind it. Some families allow each member to open one gift on Christmas eve, others wait until Christmas morning when the youngest child distributes the gifts.

Traditions are intricately woven into almost every aspect of the holiday. In our family growing up we enjoyed any number of traditions. One that might sound a bit odd to most persons was an activity that my entire family participated in every year while we were growing up. Each holiday season, typically a week prior to Christmas, we would load up the family into the car and drive about twenty miles over hill and valley to a small central Pennsylvania town on the far side of Altoona. Our destination was Jackson's Store where we would spend time looking at toys and Christmas decorations.

Understand that this store we journeyed to wasn't a Macy's or Nordstrom's. It wasn't even a Sears or Montgomery Ward for that matter. The best way I can describe it is a cross between Tractor Supply and a Dollar General Store. Nothing to write home about I can assure you!

Why in the world did we go there? I'm honestly not sure. Why was it special? That I do know. It became "special" and an important part of our Christmas tradition because it was something that we did as a family together! We spent time in the car on the way there talking about what we would see and, on the way home, looking at the lights on people's homes. It was special because it brought us together.

Another tradition for our family was attending Christmas Eve service at our church. This too was something we all did together as a family. How meaningful it was to be together with those you love on the most blessed night of the Christian year. Unlike the Jackson's Store experience, attending church together as a family was not something unique only to the holiday season.

But being in church together on Christmas Eve was special and important. Why? Why is it important to gather at one particular place on this most important of days?

To answer that question, we need to travel in our minds back to ancient Jerusalem. In that city there was a temple built by a great King (Solomon). To many it was understood to be the holiest place in all the world. It was to this temple that all good Jews traveled to worship God. In fact, it was believed that this was the only true place where the presence of the Lord God Almighty could be felt and experienced. The presence of this temple was symbolic of the presence of God in the lives of the Jewish people.

Eventually, however, enemies defeated the Jews and destroyed their temple. All that remained was a portion of the western wall of the temple grounds. It stands to this very day and we know it as the Western or Wailing Wall. The wall is still considered by the

Jewish people be perhaps the holiest place in all the world. It is the only remaining portion of the temple which again, signifies the presence of God in the lives of the people of God.

A tradition developed over time of coming to that great wall and placing one's hand upon it and offering a prayer. Millions of Jews and Christians alike do this every year. Some persons write prayers on pieces of paper, roll them up and stick them in the wall.

For many this is a once in a lifetime experience. Several years ago as I stood before that very same wall I remember praying for peace in this world and that the love of Christ might fill the hearts of all people. That same day hundreds, maybe thousands of others stood at that same wall praying for special needs they had while still others were giving thanks for things they had already received. The common thread that bound us all together was that we had come to be with God.

When we attend worship on Christmas Eve or Christmas Day, we do so because it is our tradition. Perhaps for some it is little more than just that. But just maybe we also gather because we know that one night two thousand years ago in a faraway land, a baby was born of humble parents and in meager surroundings with but a handful of others even taking note. That child changed the world and changed our lives forever. He lived and grew and preached and healed and showed us that we must love one another and forgive one another and help one another in his name. And when he died on a cross, he did so that we might live. Much of what we do this season is out of tradition but let us also do so with a deep respect and attitude of thanksgiving for the gift of salvation he has brought to us.

Attending Christmas worship reminds us that we must be his faithful followers not only one hour on the 24th of December but every hour of every day of the year. In this ever-changing world in which religious beliefs are mocked, where religious expression of any kind often is discouraged, and where wishing another a "Merry Christmas" has been replaced by the more politically correct "Happy Non-Sectarian, Non-religiously Affiliated Holiday", we run the risk of literally taking CHRIST completely out of Christmas.

But as offensive as I find the fact that nativity scenes and Christmas carols and crosses and the like are regularly removed in favor of a more secular celebration of the season, what is even more upsetting to me is that those of us who claim to believe in and follow the Christ child do all that we can to minimize Christ's influence on us not only during the holiday season but year round.

Seriously consider the following questions; Have you really felt Christ in your life this past year? Have you once experienced a difficulty and come through it? If so how did you honor or thank Jesus for that gift? Perhaps you're hurting this moment. Maybe you have suffered a loss or are troubled. Have you asked Christ to enter your life and help you with the burden you are carrying? Please know that you can, and He will!

Do you have a wish or a prayer for your friends or family, or for this troubled world in which we will live? Have you taken it to God in prayer believing that what you ask can indeed come to pass? This year remember the light of the world enters our lives; a light that brightens and warms and comforts all who draw near. That same light is given to us to share this holiday season. I encourage you to create or continue one new tradition in your home this season. Share your life, your love and your relationship to Christ with others. Why not make it a new tradition?

> **Prayer:** God of the Silent Night, bring us together this year with those that mean the most to us. But keep us also mindful of those who are lonely and are counting on us to bring the Light of Christ into their hearts. As we reach the end of this year's Advent journey, help us to hold the memories we have unpacked close to our hearts, passing them along to those closest to us. God is with us! Amen.

Musical Reflection: "Silent Night"

Scan the QR Code below to hear the Musical Reflection

JANET LORD grew up in the small town of Creighton, Pennsylvania and still lives in the house built by her great-grandparents. Along with being in constant need of repairs, it is full of tangible and intangible memories. She has a degree in Music Education from Indiana University of Pennsylvania and received her theological education through Wesley Seminary in Washington, D.C. She is a permanent, ordained, Deacon in the Global Methodist Church, serving as the Secretary of the newly formed Allegheny West Provisional Conference. She is Mom to Tim, official Aunt to Megan, and unofficial Aunt to countless others.

MARK HECHT is a lifelong resident of Pennsylvania. He has lived and served in rural areas of the commonwealth and also in some of the most urban and inner-city settings as well. He holds degrees from Allegheny College, Pittsburgh Theological Seminary and Wesley Theological Seminary. In addition to thirty-five years of parish ministry, he has served as a hospice chaplain and a professor of church history at several universities. Mark is an ordained Elder in the Global Methodist Church, serving as the Senior Pastor of First Methodist Church in Warren, PA and as a Presiding Elder in the newly formed Allegheny West Provisional Conference of the Global Methodist Church. Mark and his wife of thirty-five years, Karen have four adult children and four grandchildren.

Made in the USA
Middletown, DE
29 June 2023